✧ *Companions for the Journey* ✧

Praying with
Hildegard of Bingen

✧ *Companions for the Journey* ✧

Praying with Hildegard of Bingen

by
Gloria Durka

Saint Mary's Press
Christian Brothers Publications
Winona, Minnesota

For wise women everywhere,
especially two cherished friends—
✧ *Sister Mary Angelica Bielska, CSSF,* ✧
and in memoriam
✧ *Mary Ann Dunworth McMahon—* ✧
of each of whom it can be said:

Lo, here is one who will increase our loves.
—Dante Alighieri

The publishing team included Carl Koch, development editor; Cheryl Driv-dahl, copy editor; Maura C. Goessling, production editor and typesetter; Elaine Kohner, illustrator; pre-press, printing, and binding by the graphics division of Saint Mary's Press.

The acknowledgments continue on page 112.

Printed in the United States of America

Printing: 10 9 8 7 6

Year: 2001 00 99 98

ISBN 0-88489-254-9

✧ Contents ✧

✧ Foreword ✧

Companions for the Journey

Just as food is required for human life, so are companions. Indeed, the word *companions* comes from two Latin words: *com,* meaning "with," and *panis,* meaning "bread." Companions nourish our heart, mind, soul, and body. They are also the people with whom we can celebrate the sharing of bread.

Perhaps the most touching stories in the Bible are about companionship: the Last Supper, the wedding feast at Cana, the sharing of the loaves and the fishes, and Jesus' breaking of bread with the disciples on the road to Emmaus. Each incident of companionship with Jesus revealed more about his mercy, love, wisdom, suffering, and hope. When Jesus went to pray in the Garden of Olives, he craved the companionship of the Apostles. They let him down. But God sent the Spirit to inflame the hearts of the Apostles, and they became faithful companions to Jesus and to each other.

Throughout history, other faithful companions have followed Jesus and the Apostles. These saints and mystics have also taken the journey from conversion, through suffering, to resurrection. Just as they were inspired by the holy people who went before them, so too may you take them as your companions as you walk on your spiritual journey.

The Companions for the Journey series is a response to the spiritual hunger of Christians. This series makes available the rich spiritual teachings of mystics and guides whose wisdom can help us on our pilgrimages. As you complete the last meditation in each volume, it is hoped that you will feel supported, challenged, and affirmed by a soul-companion on your spiritual journey.

The spiritual hunger that has emerged over the last twenty years is a great sign of renewal in Christian life. People fill retreat programs and workshops on topics in spirituality. The demand for spiritual directors exceeds the number available. Interest in the lives and writings of saints and mystics is increasing as people search for models of whole and holy Christian life.

Praying with Hildegard

Praying with Hildegard of Bingen is more than just a book about Hildegard's spirituality. This book seeks to engage you in praying in the way that Hildegard did about issues and themes that were central to her experience. Each meditation can enlighten your understanding of her spirituality and lead you to reflect on your own experience.

The goal of *Praying with Hildegard of Bingen* is that you will discover Hildegard's profound spirituality and integrate her spirit and wisdom into your relationship with God, with your brothers and sisters, and with your own heart and mind.

Suggestions for Praying with Hildegard

Meet Hildegard of Bingen, a courageous and fascinating companion for your pilgrimage, by reading the introduction to this book, which begins on page 15. It provides a brief biography of Hildegard and an outline of the major themes of her spirituality.

Once you meet Hildegard, you will be ready to pray with her and to encounter God, your sisters and brothers, and yourself in new and wonderful ways. To help your prayer, here are some suggestions that have been part of the tradition of Christian spirituality:

Create a sacred space. Jesus said, "When you pray, go to your private room, shut yourself in, and so pray to your [God] who is in that secret place, and your [God] who sees all that is done in secret will reward you" (Matthew 6:6). Solitary prayer is best done in a place where you can have privacy and silence, both of which can be luxuries in the life of busy people. If privacy and silence are not possible, create a quiet, safe place within yourself, perhaps while riding to and from work, while sitting in line at the dentist's office, or while waiting for someone. Do the best you can, knowing that a loving God is present everywhere. Whether the meditations in this book are used for solitary prayer or with a group, try to create a prayerful mood with candles, meditative music, an open Bible, or a crucifix.

Open yourself to the power of prayer. Every human experience has a religious dimension. All of life is suffused with God's presence. So remind yourself that God is present as you begin your period of prayer. Do not worry about distractions. If something keeps intruding during your prayer, spend some time talking with God about it. Be flexible because God's Spirit blows where it will.

Prayer can open your mind and widen your vision. Be open to new ways of seeing God, people, and yourself. As you open yourself to the Spirit of God, different emotions are evoked, such as sadness from tender memories, or joy from a celebration recalled. Our emotions are messages from God that can tell us much about our spiritual quest. Also, prayer strengthens our will to act. Through prayer, God can touch our will and empower us to live according to what we know is true.

Finally, many of the meditations in this book will call you to employ your memories, your imagination, and the circumstances of your life as subjects for prayer. The great mystics and saints realized that they had to use all their resources to know God better. Indeed, God speaks to us continually and touches us constantly. We must learn to listen and feel with all the means that God has given us.

Come to prayer with an open mind, heart, and will.

Preview each meditation before beginning. After you have placed yourself in God's presence, spend a few moments previewing the readings and especially the reflection activities. Several reflection activities are given in each meditation because different styles of prayer appeal to different personalities or personal needs. **Note that each meditation has more**

reflection activities than can be done during one prayer period. Therefore, select only one or two reflection activities each time you use a meditation. Do not feel compelled to complete all the reflection activities.

Read meditatively. Each meditation offers you a story about Hildegard and a reading from her writings. Take your time reading. If a particular phrase touches you, stay with it. Relish its feelings, meanings, and concerns.

Use the reflections. Following the readings is a short reflection in commentary form, which is meant to give perspective to the readings. Then you are offered several ways of meditating on the readings and the theme of the prayer. You may be familiar with the different methods of meditating, but in case you are not, they are described briefly here:

✦ *Repeated short prayer or mantra:* One means of focusing your prayer is to use a *mantra*, or "prayer word." The mantra may be a single word or a short phrase taken from the readings or from the Scriptures. For example, a mantra for a meditation on living in light might be "come, Living Light" or "Light." Repeated slowly in harmony with your breathing, the mantra helps you center your heart and mind on one action or attribute of God.

✦ *Lectio divina:* This type of meditation is "divine studying," a concentrated reflection on the word of God or the wisdom of a spiritual writer. Most often in *lectio divina,* you will be invited to read one of the passages several times and then concentrate on one or two sentences, pondering their meaning for you and their effect on you. *Lectio divina* commonly ends with formulation of a resolution.

✦ *Guided meditation:* In this type of meditation, our imagination helps us consider alternative actions and likely consequences. Our imagination helps us experience new ways of seeing God, our neighbors, ourselves, and nature. When Jesus told his followers parables and stories, he engaged their imagination. In this book, you will be invited to follow guided meditations.

One way of doing a guided meditation is to read the scene or story several times, until you know the outline and can recall it when you enter into reflection. Or before your prayer time, you may wish to record the meditation on a tape recorder. If so, remember to allow pauses for reflection between phrases and to speak with a slow, peaceful pace and tone. Then, during prayer, when you have finished the readings and the reflection commentary, you can turn on your recording of the meditation and be led through it. If you find your own voice too distracting, ask a friend to make the tape for you.

✦ *Examen of consciousness:* The reflections often will ask you to examine how God has been speaking to you in your past and present experience—in other words, the reflections will ask you to examine your awareness of God's presence in your life.

✦ *Journal writing:* Writing is a process of discovery. If you write for any length of time, stating honestly what is on your mind and in your heart, you will unearth much about who you are, how you stand with your God, what deep longings reside in your soul, and more. In some reflections, you will be asked to write a dialog with Jesus or someone else. If you have never used writing as a means of meditation, try it. Reserve a special notebook for your journal writing. If desired, you can go back to your entries at a future time for an examen of consciousness.

✦ *Action:* Occasionally, a reflection will suggest singing a favorite hymn, going out for a walk, or undertaking some other physical activity. Actions can be meaningful forms of prayer.

Using the Meditations for Group Prayer

If you wish to use the meditations for community prayer, these suggestions may help:

✦ Read the theme to the group. Call the community into the presence of God, using the short opening prayer. Invite one or two participants to read one or both readings. If you use both readings, observe the pause between them.

✦ The reflection commentary may be used as a reading, or it can be deleted, depending on the needs and interests of the group.

✦ Select one of the reflection activities for your group. Allow sufficient time for your group to reflect, to recite a centering prayer or mantra, to accomplish a studying prayer *(lectio divina)*, or to finish an examen of consciousness. Depending on the group and the amount of available time, you may want to invite the participants to share their reflections, responses, or petitions with the group.

✦ Reading the passage from the Scriptures may serve as a summary of the meditation.

✦ If a formulated prayer or a psalm is given as a closing, it may be recited by the entire group. Or you may ask participants to offer their own prayers for the closing.

Now you are ready to begin praying with Hildegard of Bingen, a faithful and caring companion on this stage of your spiritual journey. Hildegard has inspired many people to seek a closer relationship with God. It is hoped that you will find her to be a true soul-companion.

CARL KOCH
Editor

✧ **Preface** ✧

To take a journey is to make a trip toward a place. Although the final destination is not always clear to us, we know when we do finally arrive. Probing Saint Hildegard of Bingen's life and works can seem like traveling in many directions at once because many possibilities beckon to us. The paths Hildegard shows us are like so many sparkling rivers that promise to carry us. I have found her spirit spilled onto the pages of her writings and the places wherein she dwelt. My hope is that you can do likewise through the pages of this humble work. And so, I invite you to join me in an adventure to discover some of the wonders of Hildegard's spirituality so that we might be nourished by her wisdom to do as she did—live passionately into the future, whose destination is the Center.

I am grateful to Sister Ancilla Ferlings, OSB, of the Abbey of Saint Hildegard, Eibingen, for her generous hospitality and willingness to share with me her insights into the significance of Hildegard for contemporary times. Special thanks also to Clevie Youngblood, RSHM, who typed the final manuscript with such great care.

In the company of Hildegard, let us begin.

GLORIA DURKA
Feast of Hildegard of Bingen
17 September 1990

✧ Introduction ✧

The Prophetess of the Rhine

Except in Germany, the name Hildegard of Bingen meant little to Christians until recently. This story provides some explanation for the interest in this twelfth-century abbess, prophetess, healer, preacher, and mystic:

> Some years ago, wrote the monk Guibert to his friend Radulfus, strange and incredible rumors had reached his ears at the Belgian monastery of Gembloux. They concerned an old woman, abbess of the recent Benedictine foundation at Bingen-am-Rhein, who had gained such fame that multitudes flocked to her convent, from curiosity or devotion, to seek her prophecies and prayers. All who returned thence astonished their hearers, but none could give a plausible account of the woman, save only that her soul was "said to be illumined by an invisible splendor known to her alone." Finally Guibert, impatient with rumor and zealous for the truth, resolved to find out for himself. In the year 1175 he wrote to this famous seer, Hildegard, with mingled curiosity and awe. . . . Perhaps she would deign to answer a few questions about her visions. . . . As the abbess sent no reply, Guibert tried again some time later, having thought of more questions in the meantime. . . .
>
> In the end the seer favored Guibert with a reply—a detailed account of the mode of her visions—which so overwhelmed him that he declared that no woman since the Virgin Mary had received so great a gift from God. (Barbara Newman, *Sister of Wisdom*, pp. 1–2)

Who was this "old woman" and "famous seer," and how did she come to be so wise and holy? What insights and inspiration can she offer to us today?

Hildegard's Story

Her Roots

Hildegard was born into a noble German family in 1098. She was the tenth and last child of Hildebert von Bermersheim and Mechtild. When she was an infant, Hildegard's parents dedicated her to God. The promising of children to God's service was not unusual at the time. Devout parents who felt grateful for their many blessings offered one or more of their children to a monastery when they were as young as five years of age. To provide for the well-being of those children, parents frequently made generous donations during their lifetime and designated large endowments to be given to the monastery from their estates after their death. Indeed, three of Hildegard's siblings also devoted their life to the service of God: one brother was a cantor at the Mainz Cathedral, another was a cantor in Tholey, and a sister entered Hildegard's monastery.

Her Time

Hildegard entered a world still emerging from medieval chaos. With the rise of new nation-states, the twelfth century saw the birth of modern Europe. Kings united into countries lands that had long been ruled by petty nobles. Towns and cities sprang up, complete with grand Gothic cathedrals and cathedral schools. Ten years before Hildegard's birth, the University of Bologna had been founded, and ten years before her death, Oxford became a university. Although scholarship began to flourish, anyone deviating from church teaching had to beware. In the early part of the twelfth century, heretics were burned at Cologne; by the end of the century, civil authorities began to utilize the tribunal practice of the Inquisition to bring order among their people.

Hildegard's contemporaries saw thousands of men march off to the Crusades. The famous Cistercian Saint Bernard of Clairvaux, with whom Hildegard corresponded, and other preachers prompted the kings of Europe to mount these disastrous expeditions against the Muslims holding the Holy Land. The Christian armies failed to win back the Holy Land, helped split the church into East and West, and saw legions of men die on foreign battlefields. On the other hand, Crusaders and merchants brought back knowledge, inventions, and goods from the Middle and Far East.

Considerable confusion ravaged the church. Many monasteries had grown lax in the observance of their rule. While Hildegard was alive, thirteen popes and twelve antipopes claimed the chair of Peter. The Holy Roman emperors and the reigning popes frequently argued over matters in which jurisdiction between church and state seemed unclear. For example, Pope Alexander III and Holy Roman Emperor Frederick Barbarossa battled continually until they signed the Peace of Venice ending Frederick's support of three antipopes. At one point during Hildegard's lifetime, Frederick even ordered the destruction of monasteries supporting the Roman pontiff.

Her Life Under Jutta's Care

When Hildegard was eight years old, her parents entrusted her to the tutelage of Jutta of Sponheim, an anchoress who lived in a hermitage next to the thriving monastery of men at Disibodenberg. Besides tutoring Hildegard in practical skills, Jutta taught her to read the Latin Bible, especially the Psalms, and to chant the Divine Office. Jutta not only was Hildegard's mentor but grew to be her closest friend. Their friendship flourished for thirty years until Jutta's death. Entrusted to Jutta at such an impressionable age, Hildegard mirrored many of Jutta's qualities.

Jutta's reputation for wisdom and virtue drew women to join her, and eventually the hermitage grew into a monastery observing the Benedictine rule. When she was mature enough as a teen, Hildegard entered the monastery and was there educated in the Benedictine traditions of music, sacred scripture, prayer, and work, such as spinning.

Her Role as Abbess

Little is known about Hildegard's life between the ages of fifteen and thirty-eight. Then, in 1136, Jutta died. Hildegard succeeded her as prioress.

Studious inquiry, prayer, art, music, and work characterized Benedictine monasteries of women. Hildegard accepted into the monastery only women of wealth or noble birth. Like most people of her time, she believed that class structure had been divinely ordained. Maintaining class structure ensured good order in society and in a monastery.

Although she exuded warmth and strength of personality that attracted the loyalty of her sisters, Hildegard's fire and determination sometimes also evoked resistance. In one of her letters, she remarked: "Several of [my sisters], looking at me with glowering eyes, would tear me to pieces behind my back, saying that they could not endure it, this insufferable hammering away of mine at the discipline of the Rule. . . . But God gave me comfort also, with other good and wise sisters, who stood by me" (Sister Anna Silvas, "Saint Hildegard of Bingen," *Tjurunga*, volume 31, p. 37). Forceful noblewoman that she was, Hildegard wanted her monastery to be an island of order and harmony in the midst of a corrupt and chaotic world.

Time passed, and Hildegard's reputation for holiness spread, drawing so many new members to the women's community at Disibodenberg that it grew too large for the space available. In 1148, Hildegard and eighteen of the nuns left Disibodenberg and founded a new abbey for women at Rupertsberg. The abbot and monks of Disibodenberg fought Hildegard at every turn, wishing to block the move. Hildegard's presence had attracted increasing numbers of pilgrims, with their donations, to the monastery. At one point in Hildegard's correspondence with the abbot, she compared his style with that of "a grumbling bear, a glum and bungling ass, and birds who fly neither high nor low" (Miriam Schmitt, "Saint Hildegard of Bingen: Leaven of God's Justice," *Cistercian Studies*, volume 24, p. 76). Even though tensions remained between the men's community and the nuns at Rupertsberg, Hildegard managed to establish her new monastery and, through contracts, set it on a firm legal footing.

The community blossomed. By 1165, the number of nuns exceeded the capacity of the house at Rupertsberg, so Hildegard founded another abbey at Eibingen. Hildegard's creative output, in the main, dates from the time of her move to Rupertsberg.

The Benedictine Way of Life

To understand Hildegard requires some understanding of the Benedictine way of life. As Hildegard's biographers indicate, life on Mount Saint Rupert maintained a quiet harmony. The monastic discipline made life well-ordered and secure, a balanced rhythm of prayer, work, and study. Seven periods divided the day. The first began at 2:00 a.m. with the chanting of nocturns. After returning to sleep for a short while, the sisters rose again before 6:00 a.m. to chant lauds. After this, they spent some time in private reading or meditation in their cell, then returned to chapel to recite prime. A simple breakfast followed, and then a brief period of morning work in the laundry, in the kitchen, or at housekeeping chores.

The sisters gathered in the chapel again to recite terce and participate in the eucharistic liturgy, usually sung by the entire community. After liturgy, the sisters did manual labor in the herb garden, the vineyards, or the vestry. Before noon, they chanted sext, and then they ate lunch.

After the midday meal, the sisters rested briefly. Then, at around 3:00 p.m., they gathered to sing none, following which they worked again at various jobs. After a light supper and the chanting of vespers, the nuns read, studied, and meditated before ending their day by chanting compline together.

By day's end, Hildegard and her sisters had worked about six hours, slept eight hours, and prayed together three or four hours. The rest of the day had been spent in spiritual reading, study, and meditation. All in all, the sisters aspired to live in harmony with God, humankind, and themselves.

This care for harmony included care for their physical needs. Unusual for her time, Hildegard advocated warm baths and nutritional food both as preventatives and as cures for common ailments.

In Hildegard's monastery, plumbing made water easily available for the tasks of daily hygiene. The nuns followed a plain but healthy diet. They baked their own bread and ate vegetables and fruit from their gardens. Hot, hearty soups warmed them on cold days, and occasionally they enjoyed cookies. Some of Hildegard's own recipes for healthy cookies still exist. All who ate helped the nuns in charge of the kitchen cleanup.

Hildegard encouraged nuns who were ill to rest adequately. Monastic life regulated fasting for all members but allowed the sick to fast only when it was necessary to cleanse the body of impurities. Hildegard earned the reputation as a healer of some repute. She actively studied medicinal herbs and the efficacy of curative treatments. People made pilgrimages to her for medical advice.

Hildegard managed the abbey cleverly and competently, making sure that the expenses needed to feed and clothe the numerous nuns and employees and the flood of guests were adequately covered. Many of the women who joined her monastery brought large dowries with them. Pilgrims seeking spiritual guidance or advice on health frequently contributed goods or money. Even so, consistent with the Benedictines' tradition, Hildegard's hospitality proved generous. And, while directing the monastery's affairs, Hildegard counseled all those who sought her help, wrote books and music, and carried on an active correspondence.

Her Visions

From early childhood, Hildegard had a deep spiritual awareness that was founded in what she later named the reflection of the Living Light. But decades passed before she understood the light and the figures that she saw in it as a gift from God. Toward the end of her life, Hildegard told her biographer that she had a vision of a dazzling light when she was about three years of age. By the time she reached her teens, Hildegard realized that no one else could see what she saw, so she stopped telling anyone about her visions.

At times, a strange luminosity filled her visual field. In this light, she perceived a variety of figures such as human forms and elaborate structures. She interpreted each figure with help from a voice from heaven. Most of the figures were images from the Hebrew Scriptures. Initially, however, Hildegard's visions baffled her. Hildegard constantly stressed that she received her visions while fully awake in mind and body.

As the visions continued, she confided them only to Jutta, who eventually reported them to the monk Volmar, her secretary. Even after Jutta's death, when Hildegard became abbess of the monastery, she did not discuss her visions.

At age forty-three, Hildegard received a prophetic call from God, commanding her, "Say and write what you see and hear" (Mother Columba Hart and Jane Bishop, trans., *Hildegard of Bingen, "Scivias,"* p. 59). This experience led her to spend ten years of industrious work composing her first book, *Scivias* (Know the ways).

However, Hildegard needed confirmation that indeed her visions came from God. She sought the advice of an abbot and the archbishop of Mainz. The archbishop was so impressed with her work that he told Pope Eugenius III about her while the pope attended a synod held in Trier in 1147–1148. The pope sent a delegation to Disibodenberg to meet Hildegard personally. The delegation returned with a positive report and a copy of *Scivias*, which the pope read to the assembled synod members.

At approximately this point, the great monastic reformer Bernard of Clairvaux endorsed Hildegard's visions in conversation with Eugenius. One of Hildegard's biographers commented: "The Pope was advised, (lest so remarkable a light should, through silence, remain hidden), that if the Lord manifested at this time so great a favour, it ought to be confirmed by papal authority. At which, Eugenius sent the blessed maiden a letter of encouragement in which he included permission, with his official protection" (Sister Anna Silvas, "Translation: The Life of Saint Hildegard," *Tjurunga*, volume 29, p. 25; hereafter cited as "Life"). A series of letters between Hildegard and Pope Eugenius III followed. The pope's approbation not only increased Hildegard's self-confidence, but it also gave her authentication in the public realm. Her vocation as prophetess was born.

Her Public Ministry

Eventually, Hildegard's reputation as a prophetess, adviser, and healer spread far beyond the Rhineland. People came from far-off regions to Rupertsberg to consult with her. Hildegard became a counselor to popes, emperors, and people in all walks of life. She advised popes Anastasius IV, Adrian IV, and Eugenius III and exchanged correspondence with, among others, Henry II of England, Eleanor of Aquitaine, and the Byzantine empress Irene. Hildegard showed keen awareness of the political and scholarly developments of her era.

To civil rulers, Hildegard constantly preached justice in the exercise of their authority. Hildegard counseled the clergy against worldliness. She urged them to be true to their vocation as spiritual leaders and models of virtue. Of particular concern to her were abuses in three areas: simony (the purchase or sale of a church office or ecclesiastical preferment), clerical celibacy, and the subservience that church prelates paid to secular powers. In Germany, Emperor Frederick Barbarossa virtually ruled the church. Many bishops had become his lackeys.

Hildegard also traveled, preaching to clergy, laity, nuns, monks, and ecclesial officials in monasteries and churches throughout the Rhineland. Despite persistent frail health, she undertook four extended preaching tours between 1155 and 1171.

In her sermons, Hildegard sometimes likened the church to a beautiful woman, dressed and bejeweled magnificently, who had been smeared with mud and violated, and now wailed to heaven in her misery. Like the prophets of the Hebrew Scriptures, Hildegard proclaimed that sin and corruption destroyed the harmony of the cosmos, besmirching the grandeur of God's creation. The harmony of the universe as created by God sounded like that of a grand symphony; sin threw discord into the music of the spheres, and sinners would suffer divine judgment. Hildegard took church leaders to task, exhorting against greed, fornication, negligence, and oppression. So powerful was her preaching that devout listeners collected the texts of her sermons.

Her fame caused Emperor Frederick Barbarossa to invite Hildegard to meet with him at his palace in Ingelheim. She accepted. No record of their conversation exists, but several years after this meeting, Frederick granted the Rupertsberg monastery an edict of imperial protection in perpetuity. Even when Frederick ordered attacks on other monasteries because they supported the Roman pope over Frederick's appointed antipopes, the Rupertsberg abbey remained safe. Despite receiving Frederick's favor during all his wrangling with the legitimate popes, Hildegard wrote Frederick strong letters of protest about his treatment of the Vatican and the rightful successors of Peter.

Another wonderful example of Hildegard's moral courage occurred the year before she died. The choirbishop of Mainz and the archbishop placed Hildegard, in her eighties, and her sisters of Rupertsberg under an interdict for burying a revolutionary youth in their monastery cemetery. An interdict prohibits those censored from receiving most of the sacraments and being given a Christian burial. Thus, the Eucharist could not be celebrated, nor communion received, nor the Divine Office sung in the abbey. Still, Hildegard refused to dig up the body and eject it from her monastery grounds, insisting that the youth had confessed, had been anointed, and had communicated before dying. To prevent the choir chapter of Mainz from digging up the body themselves, Hildegard personally went to the cemetery and removed all traces of the burial. In her letter to the archbishop, Hildegard lamented how, by the interdiction, he had silenced the most wonderful music on the Rhine. Eventually, the interdict was removed. Hildegard's courage won out. She died shortly thereafter.

Legends tell that when Hildegard died on 17 September 1179, two streams of light appeared in the skies and crossed over the room in which she was dying, an appropriate death for one nourished by the Living Light throughout her life. In Hildegard's passing into eternal life, a brief glimpse of that light was made manifest to all who witnessed her entrance into glory.

Hildegard's Writings

Hildegard left a remarkable legacy: nearly three hundred letters to nuns, rulers, bishops, and nobles; dozens of poems; and nine books, three of which were major theological works. Among her books were one on physiology (*Physica*) and one on health (*Causae et Curae*). She was the author of an interpretation of the *Rule of Saint Benedict*, a commentary on the Gospels, a commentary on the Saint Athanasian Creed, and two biographies of saints. In addition, she wrote music for use in the monastery. Her compositions included seventy-seven songs and a liturgical drama.

Of the many works by Hildegard, *Scivias* is probably best known. It provides the reader with a comprehensive guide to Christian doctrine and then ends with an apocalyptic section, a group of hymns, and a morality play—by far the oldest example of this type.

Hildegard was not a systematic theologian: "The substance of her world-view was *revealed*, not acquired through study. Her spirit being as creative and intuitive as it was, she brings a freshness to everything she touches, as if it were being approached for the first time" (Silvas, "Saint Hildegard," *Tjurunga*, volume 29, p. 12). Hildegard related that God commanded her to write down the revelations she received.

Hildegard's Spirituality

Looking at Hildegard's life is like looking through a kaleidoscope. At each turn, we see new facets of a complex life, lived between delight and struggle and between her vast knowledge and her profound sense of mystery.

The sharpest and clearest lens we can use to understand Hildegard's spirituality is the Benedictine rule. Above all, Hildegard was a Benedictine, imbued with the love of the Divine Office with its spirit of communal praise and use of song. Formed in their spirituality by the rule of Saint Benedict, Benedictines fostered contemplation through meditation, study, and prayer based on the mystery of Christ experienced in scripture and liturgical worship. This contemplative focus was part of Hildegard's heritage.

For Hildegard, holiness flowered in a monastic life of obedience and communal prayer. By following the rule of life with its rhythmic movement between prayer, work, study, and meditation, a person would acquire the spiritual strength and virtue to engage in the struggle against evil. Typical to people of her time, Hildegard viewed God and Satan as engaged in a cosmic, spiritual war. The discipline, order, and simple life of the monastery armed Hildegard and her sisters to battle on the side of God.

Hildegard's Spiritual Legacy for Today

What is so attractive about Hildegard's spirituality today? It seems to fill a vacuum in the heart and mind of people who are journeying toward the center of life. Hildegard provides wonderful and inspiring insights into friendship, living with conflict, relying on God, seeking the Light, and the beauty of a virtuous life. But several elements of Hildegard's spirituality particularly explain her unique appeal:

✦ *An ecological perspective:* Hildegard's writings reflect her profound sense of being related to the earth. Unlike some of her contemporaries who rejected earthly life as binding their spirit, Hildegard believed this earth was home and a region of delight, and as such must be admired, cherished, and protected. One modern commentator concluded: "For her, the fundamental sin is, so to speak, 'ecological'. That is, it consists in a rupture in the inter-relationship and interdependence of the whole of creation. For her, liberation from sin means a re-establishment of the harmony of the original creation, the assumption by every human being of their co-creative responsibility with God for the earth" (Silvas, "Saint Hildegard," *Tjurunga,* volume 29, p. 15)

✦ *An emphasis on the beauty of a life of justice and compassion:* For Hildegard, holiness implied acting justly and doing good works. Like an orchard that bears good fruit, virtuous lives produce good work, having a power for *viriditas,* or "greenness" (Hart and Bishop, *"Scivias,"* p. 90). A lifestyle of good works requires awareness of the times, discernment of the good, choice as to course of action, and taking of action. Such a just and compassionate life shines forth in beauty.

✦ *An invitation to a holistic use of our intelligence:* Hildegard's style of writing is fascinating and at times difficult because she used an intricate array of metaphors and rich symbols. From a literary perspective, the biblical prophets were the only authors who directly influenced her style. The wonderful images that she employed invite readers to taste and see the goodness of God by nurturing the analytic and metaphoric modes of perception. The writings of Hildegard prime our imagination and touch our intuition.

✦ *A mystical theology grounded in the integrity of creation:* Hildegard experienced God living in and through all of creation, but she did not collapse the identities of God and creation or dismiss their differences. In one of her visions, God declared:

> "I am the breeze
> that nurtures all things
> green.
> . . . I am the rain
> coming from the dew
> that causes the grasses to laugh
> with joy of life.
> . . . I am the yearning for good."

(Gabriele Uhlein, *Meditations with Hildegard of Bingen,* p. 31)

✦ *A powerful role model for women to be true to their own religious experience:* Hildegard reflected and wrote at length about the experience of women. Her correspondence reveals a lifestyle of political and social activism. Hildegard actively challenged the status quo. She now challenges all women to respect their own experience, to affirm their talents and skills, and to transform the world in authentic partnership with men.

Hildegard wrote and preached, healed and sang God's praises, always desiring to bring the earth and humankind into closer harmony with God's wonderful design at the creation of the world. Corruption and disharmony wrack our world just as they did hers. Her call to bind the wounds of the earth, to live justly and compassionately, to cocreate with God makes her a stirring and challenging companion for the spiritual journey.

✧ Meditation 1 ✧

Living in Light

Theme: From the time she was a little girl, Hildegard experienced God as living light.

Opening prayer: My God, you are the living light of the world.

About Hildegard

At the beginning of her book *Scivias*, Hildegard described her experience of the Living Light:

> It happened that, in the eleven hundred and forty-first year of the Incarnation of the Son of God, Jesus Christ, when I was forty-two years and seven months old, Heaven was opened and a fiery light of exceeding brilliance came and permeated my whole brain, and inflamed my whole heart and my whole breast, not like a burning but like a warming flame, as the sun warms anything its rays touch. And immediately I knew the meaning of the exposition of the Scriptures, namely the Psalter, the Gospel and the other catholic volumes of both the Old and the New Testaments, though I did not have the interpretation of the words of their texts or the division of the syllables or the knowledge of cases or tenses. But I had sensed in

myself wonderfully the power and mystery of secret and admirable visions from my childhood—that is, from the age of five—up to that time, as I do now. This, however, I showed to no one except a few religious persons who were living in the same manner as I. (Hart and Bishop, "*Scivias*," pp. 59–60)

Pause: Ponder this question: Have I ever experienced God as warm and revealing light?

Hildegard's Words

The sun rises in the east and becomes stronger and stronger in its incandescence in the south. But after the sun has reached its midday position, it begins to decline and thus completes its course until the next morning. And because the sun does not penetrate the north, it is cold on Earth toward morning and evening.

[Here, Hildegard quoted God's revelation to her:] *But I, who am without beginning, am the fire by which all the stars are enkindled. I am the light that covers the dark places so that they cannot grasp the light. Therefore, light does not mingle with the dark places, and therefore the darkness does not come to the light.*

Thus human beings, too, have been created by God to have a good conscience, which is the light of truth. And just as those who have an evil conscience, which is an empty space without enduring merit or reward, are inclined to evil, we see that heaven and Earth, that is, light and darkness, are indicated in human beings. (P. 106)

Then God created us in the light of divine power. . . . God is the living light in every respect. From God all lights shine. Therefore, we remain a light that gives off light through God. (Matthew Fox, ed., *Hildegard of Bingen's Book of Divine Works with Letters and Songs*, pp. 170–171)

Reflection

In her attempt to describe God's transcendence and yet permeating presence, God's mystery and yet constant revelations, Hildegard filled her writings with images of God as light. God was not remote, but inexhaustible.

God's light does more than illuminate our soul; it draws us to recognize that the entire cosmos manifests the Creator. Just as the sun lights us on our way, so anything that shows us the way to God is "light." For Hildegard, faith in God was a way of knowing God as revealed in the light God shed throughout the cosmos and throughout ourselves—body and spirit.

In days of old, the Law of Moses lighted the way for believers; now the light is Jesus the Christ. Intimately knowledgeable of scripture, Hildegard believed in and resonated with Jesus, who announced: "I am the light of the world; anyone who follows me will not be walking in the dark but will have the light of life" (John 8:12). She also understood that revelation summons us to respond to it in action. All those who follow Jesus let the light of God's own goodness shine out through them.

✦ God's inspiration and care came to Hildegard as a warming flame. Light a candle. Sit before the flame, and let it warm you. Spend a few moments observing how the flame flickers with the movement of air. Can you recall any times when candles gave you comfort? Perhaps during a storm when the electrical power went out? Maybe while observing a pious person lighting a votive lamp at some shrine in a church corner? Or maybe when you lighted a candle as a symbol of your own trust in God's sustaining love?

Recall some other occasions during which candles are used, such as to complete a table setting before a meal. And remember why this form of light is an especially appropriate way of transforming an ordinary act into one that is extraordinary. Why can warm light bring with it contentment and security?

As you sit before your candle, if you feel inclined, pray "Your love, my God, is true and lasting warmth" or a short prayer phrase of your own. Repeat the prayer slowly, calmly, letting the words soothe you.

✧ Light symbolizes illumination and understanding: enlightenment. God's warm light gave Hildegard a profound comprehension of the truths of God's word. Talk to God about areas of your life in which no light seems to be shining. Ask God to send light into these areas of incomprehension and misunderstanding.

✧ The light of Christ also energizes, giving us courage to love and to proclaim God's word. In what areas of your life do you need the light that gives courage? Discuss with Jesus your need for the flame of passion and strength.

✧ We especially appreciate light when we first experience darkness, maybe because darkness reminds us of our vulnerability to evil or pain. As an act of trust, repeat these words from scripture: "Darkness is passing away / and the true light is already shining" (1 John 2:8). Offer this prayer often throughout the day.

God's Word

You are light for the world. A city built on a hill-top cannot be hidden. No one lights a lamp to put it under a tub; they put it on the lamp-stand where it shines for everyone in the house. In the same way your light must shine in people's sight, so that, seeing your good works, they may give praise to [God, our creator]. (Matthew 5:14–16)

Closing prayer: O God, help me always to see the light in the darkness, so that I may be a light for my sisters and brothers.

✧ **Meditation 2** ✧

A Feather on the Breath of God

Theme: Hildegard never ceased to be amazed at how God showered her with so much grace and light. She realized that God, who is the source of novelty and creativity, sustains all life with inexhaustible energy.

Opening prayer: "Great are you, Yahweh, and most worthy of praise; / your greatness is beyond our understanding" (Psalm 145:3).

About Hildegard

Hildegard's courage and energy inspired awe in her contemporaries. Besides founding two monasteries, composing music, and providing spiritual counsel and direction for her sisters and other people, she wrote volumes.

Wondering about the sources of her inspiration, the monk Guibert of Gembloux, Belgium, wrote to Hildegard when she was seventy-seven years old, asking: "Do these visions speak to you in Latin or German?" and "Does your knowledge of the Bible come through study or only through the action of the Holy Spirit?" (Fox, *Book of Divine Works*, p. 347). When he received no answer the first time, Guibert wrote to Hildegard a second time.

Eventually, Hildegard answered the persistent Guibert:

God works where God wills, for the honor of the divine name and not for the honor of earth-bound mortals. But I am continuously filled with fear and trembling. For I do not recognize in myself security through any kind of personal ability. And yet I raise my hands aloft to God, that I might be held by God, just like a feather which has no weight from its own strength and lets itself be carried by the wind. (Fox, *Book of Divine Works*, p. 348)

Given God's intimate revelations to her, Hildegard knew that God carries us through life, ever gracefully, if unpredictably.

Guibert became so excited when he received Hildegard's letter that he read her words to his whole community.

Pause: Reflect on the image of yourself as a feather and of God as the wind, carrying you along.

Hildegard's Words

Fiery Spirit,
fount of courage,
life within life
of all that has being!

. . . .

O sacred breath O blazing
love O savor in the breast and balm
flooding the heart with
the fragrance of good,

O limpid mirror of God
who leads wanderers
home and hunts out the lost,

. . . .

O current of power permeating all
in the heights upon the earth and
in all deeps:
you bind and gather
all people together.

Out of you clouds
come streaming, winds
take wing from you, dashing
rain against stone;
and ever-fresh springs
well from you, washing
the evergreen globe.

O teacher of those who know,
a joy to the wise
is the breath of Sophia.

Praise then be yours!
you are the song of praise,
the delight of life,
a hope and a potent honor
granting garlands of light.

(Barbara Newman, trans., "Sequence for the Holy Spirit,"
in *Saint Hildegard of Bingen, "Symphonia,"* pp. 149–151)

Reflection

The realization that God worked in her life sustained Hildegard through all her struggles and frequent bouts of physical illness. Hildegard derived strength from doing what she felt God was inviting her to do. When she hesitated or resisted, the storms of emotions or her physical illness grew worse.

Our spiritual health and physical health are intertwined. Our life is spent in growing more aware of who we are in relation to ourselves, to other creatures, and to God. Yet, we often become distracted from the realization that God's grace is ever unfolding and lifting us up. Our energy and courage for the journey to the center of reality waxes and wanes. If we could keep the fact of God's sustaining love clearly before us, the journey would seem less frightening and more filled with opportunity.

❖ Read the verses in "Hildegard's Words" again slowly. Stay with a line or two that most touches you. Pray the line repeatedly, letting its meaning and feeling inspire and instruct you.

✧ Relax. Now close your eyes. Breathe deeply and slowly. Calm yourself. Then, imagine a feather being lightly carried by a gentle breeze. Notice how it dances playfully with each breeze.

How did you feel as you imagined the feather floating?

Now, try to recall any times when you felt God carrying you gently along, times when your spirit was buoyed up by the awareness of God's care for you. Give yourself plenty of time to find and cherish these moments.

✧ Can you think of another image that speaks to you of God's strength sustaining you? When are you most apt to recall this image? What are some of your other favorite images of God's sustaining love in your life?

✧ Recall a time in your life when your resilience surprised you. Thank God for this serendipitous gift. Store the memory of this gift away in a nearby part of your mind. Have it ready for use during hard times.

✧ Make a list of some difficult tasks, painful confrontations, and hard choices you might have to undergo in the future. When you are finished, lift up your hands and turn each of these items into a prayer. You may wish to offer each difficulty to God as a prayer for strength. Or you may wish to restate each item as an affirmation of your belief that God will carry you through. For example, with your hands uplifted, you might say, "I pray for your strength, O God, to carry me through my move to a new home (or my change of work, or my recovery from surgery)."

God's Word

With God for us, no one can stand against us. God even gave Jesus, God's own son, for the liberation of us all. Since God made such a complete gift, we can be assured of God's free gift to us. Nothing can tear us from the love of Christ: not difficulties or despair, not prejudice, not hunger or nakedness, not insults or attacks. I am absolutely sure that neither death nor life, nothing that exists now or in the future, no power can ever stand between us and God's ever-faithful love that we have come to know in Jesus, the Christ. (Adapted from Romans 8:32,35,38–39)

Closing prayer:

O Yahweh, in your strength I am glad;
. . . .
You have granted me my heart's desire;
. . . .
For you made me a blessing forever;
you gladdened me with the joy of your presence.

(Psalm 21:1–6)

Help me remember that
I, too, am like a feather carried on your breath.
Amen.

✧ Meditation 3 ✧

The Gift of Friendship

Theme: We all hunger to feel connected to others. We need to bond with friends who love us.

Opening prayer: I pray for the grace to *see* others for who they are and to let them *be* who they are.

About Hildegard

Hildegard treasured her deep friendships. In her relationship with Jutta, she gave us a portrait of what it means to be *magistra* (teacher) and *anamchara* (soul-friend). As the years passed, Jutta and Hildegard became both teacher and soul-friend for each other.

Hildegard described Jutta as a highborn woman "inundated with the grace of God, like a river flooded by many streams" (Silvas, "Life," *Tjurunga*, volume 30, p. 70). Hildegard was among the first young girls entrusted to Jutta's care. For six years, Jutta served as Hildegard's sole *magistra*.

As a student of Jutta, Hildegard learned skills like weaving, spinning, and tending a garden. Jutta taught the young Hildegard how to prepare salves and tonics, which were praised far and wide during Hildegard's lifetime and long after her death. From Jutta, Hildegard also learned much about the nutritional value of herbs.

Hildegard trusted Jutta implicitly. In her *Vita*, Hildegard told that it was to Jutta she first revealed her visionary experiences. She did so because of Jutta's personal integrity and holiness. Jutta's most important mission as teacher and eventually as soul-friend was to help Hildegard become more thoroughly transformed by Jesus Christ. One of Hildegard's biographers, the monk Godfrey, described the time Hildegard spent with Jutta as a period of *kairos*—that is, a time of paschal journeying with Christ, so that "she might rise with him to the glory of eternal life" (Silvas, "Life," *Tjurunga*, volume 29, p. 23).

As abbess, Jutta became Hildegard's *domina*, or "appointed leader," but during the next twenty-four years, she also grew to be Hildegard's soul-friend. Indeed, Godfrey reported that as Hildegard developed in strength, wisdom, and virtue, Jutta rejoiced in her progress and began to recognize with admiration that Hildegard was flowering into "a leader and a pathfinder of the ways of excellence" (Silvas, "Life," *Tjurunga*, volume 29, p. 23).

Jutta, a true mentor, affirmed the gifts of her younger friend and follower. When Jutta died, the community bestowed its highest compliment upon her by unanimously electing Hildegard, Jutta's pre-eminent disciple for thirty years, to succeed her as their abbess. Hildegard willingly acknowledged that Jutta powerfully influenced the transformation of her life.

Pause: Ponder what the gift of friendship has meant in your life. Then, focus on what friendship means to you now.

Hildegard's Words

And it is written: "The Spirit of the Lord fills the Earth." This means that no creature, whether visible or invisible, lacks a spiritual life. And those creatures that human beings do not perceive seek their understanding until humans do perceive them. For it is from the power of the seed that the buds sprout. And it is from the buds that the fruit of the tree springs forth. (P. 281)

And now I want you to listen further to me. Those who long to bring God's words to completion must always remember that, because they are human, they are vessels of clay and so should continually focus on what they are and what they will be. . . .

. . . May God make you a mirror of life! (Fox, *Book of Divine Works*, p. 340)

Reflection

The relationship between Hildegard and Jutta moved from that of mentor and protégé to that of friends when the appropriate time came. On the spiritual journey, all of us need mentors and friends. We need mentors for their instruction and counsel, support and challenge. We need friends with whom we can give and receive consolation and affirmation, affection and acceptance. Mentors and friends help us look at ourselves as God does: as beloved, unique, and valuable creations. Jutta held up a mirror to Hildegard, fulfilling an essential part of the ministry of mentoring and friendship. In the mirror, Hildegard beheld herself as God made her.

Hildegard learned well how to be a mentor and a friend. Popes and rulers came to her for advice, and she was a true friend to the nuns in her monastery and to other people who came to know her.

✧ Recall people who have been mentors for you. List everyone of whom you can think. Then pick out the one mentor who played the most important role in helping you become the person you are now. Perhaps your mentor was a parent, a teacher, a co-worker, or a relative such as a special aunt or uncle. Ponder all the ways you have been nurtured by this special woman or man. Offer thanks to God for her or his mentoring.

✧ Bring to mind a special mentoring relationship from the Bible, and try to imagine how mentoring occurred between the two persons—for example, Elizabeth and Mary or Ruth and Naomi. Imagine some of what they may have said to each other as they shared matters of the heart.

✦ List on paper the names of your true friends. To make these friends more present, find each one's picture. Then, ponder the many ways that each friend has enhanced your life—for example, by doing the following:

✦ stretching your self-concept
✦ confirming your changes
✦ treating you kindly when you acknowledge your weakness as a "vessel of clay"

When you have finished pondering each friend, call on God's blessing for him or her.

✦ Friends hear each other into speech. Jutta empowered Hildegard's speech by listening attentively to what she said about what was in her heart. Who hears you into speech? Who do you hear into speech?

✧ Jutta taught Hildegard how to be a mentor and a friend. Then, Hildegard became a mentor and friend to other people. Many people are not empowered or affirmed until, as Hildegard said, we "perceive them."

Think about and list people for whom you are or could be a mentor. Are people calling you to mentor them? How are you responding?

Are people inviting you to befriend them? Who are they, and how are you responding?

✧ Ask the Holy Spirit that you may be "inundated with the grace of God, like a river flooded by many streams."

God's Word

You are my friends,
if you do what I command you.
I shall no longer call you servants,
because a servant does not know
[the] master's business;
I call you friends,
because I have made known to you
everything I have learnt. . . .
. . . .
My command to you
is to love one another.

(John 15:14–17)

Closing prayer: Jesus, you have shown me what it means to call another "friend." Thank you for your gift of friendship to me—your everlasting love.

✧ Meditation 4 ✧

Anointed by God's Spirit to Speak Out

Theme: Hildegard experienced herself as awakened by a great power, which enabled her to continue her life of service, inspired and guided by the Holy Spirit. Even so, confidence in her charism developed only gradually.

Opening prayer:

May the spoken words of my mouth,
the thoughts of my heart,
win favor in your sight, O Yahweh,
My Redeemer, my Rock!

(Psalm 19:14)

About Hildegard

No matter how striking the other dimensions of Hildegard's life and works, she was known best in her own time and in later ages as a prophetess. Even today, pilgrims who visit the monastery of Saint Hildegard at Eibingen, or the parish church of Saint Hildegard in the same town, will find her represented in word and illustration as Hildegard the Prophetess.

The prophetic call that Hildegard received did not free her completely from further self-doubt. For ten years, she labored over writing *Scivias*, her account of God's revelations to her.

When she finished, Hildegard wondered if anyone would take her seriously.

Hildegard decided that she needed the advice of an eminent religious figure of her time, Bernard of Clairvaux, who had initiated the reform of monastic life in Europe. In a letter, she addressed Bernard:

> Gentle father, mildest of men, I rest in your soul so that through your word you can show me, if you wish, whether I should [discuss my visions] openly or guard them in silence. For this vision causes me a lot of concern about the extent to which I should talk about what I have seen and heard. . . .
> . . . You are the eagle who gazes at the sun.
> . . . Farewell, live well in your soul and be a strong warrior for God. Amen. (Fox, *Book of Divine Works*, pp. 272–273)

Bernard not only endorsed Hildegard's writings, but recommended them to Pope Eugenius III, who read them to a meeting of bishops and then sent his official approval and personal greetings to Hildegard. From this point, Hildegard spoke more confidently of her revelations, even in public.

Indeed, Hildegard, being the true prophetess, prodded Pope Anastasius IV to clean up the corruption surrounding him in Rome. She wrote to him:

> O man, the eye of your discernment weakens; you are becoming weary, too tired to restrain the arrogant boastfulness of people to whom you have trusted your heart. . . . And why do you not cut out the roots of the evil which chokes out the good, useful, fine-tasting, sweet-smelling plants? You are neglecting justice. . . .
> . . . You who sit on the papal throne, you despise God when you don't hurl from yourself the evil but, even worse, embrace it and kiss it by silently tolerating corrupt men. . . . And you, O Rome, are like one in the throes of death. (Fox, *Book of Divine Works*, pp. 273–275)

Pause: Reflect on this question: Have I, like Hildegard, been empowered by God to proclaim God's truth and to call for conversion?

Hildegard's Words

In describing the prophets, Hildegard gave an account of her own charism:

> Who are the prophets?
> They are a royal people,
> who penetrate mystery
> and see with the spirit's eyes.
>
> In illuminating darkness they speak out.
>
> They are living, penetrating clarity.
> They are a blossom blooming only
> on the shoot that is rooted in the
> flood of light.
>
> (Uhlein, *Meditations*, p. 126)

Reflection

In the Judeo-Christian tradition, prophets serve as channels of communication between God and humankind. The Holy Spirit calls and supports prophets such as Hildegard.

Prophecy is accomplished in many ways: teaching, preaching, or writing. Prophets have vivid and rich imaginations, which allow them to discern God's actions in a constantly evolving world. Prophets also have great energy, which derives from the power of the Holy Spirit and their dedication to proclaiming God's message of justice.

Many women throughout history have prophesied. A song to celebrate Israel's crossing of the sea has been attributed to Miriam (Exodus 15:20–21). The stories about Deborah, Huldah, and Noadiah in the Hebrew Scriptures portray them as prophetesses. And in the Christian Testament, Anna was one of the first people to proclaim Jesus as the Messiah (Luke 2:36–38). Hildegard acknowledged the company of these women who prophesied.

Hildegard's prophecy promised that God will never abandon us. God will never stop giving us another chance to enter into a new relationship with God. And this just may be the greatest prophecy of all: good will win over evil. Hildegard challenges us to give the same message through our love for one another and our proclamation of God's good news.

✧ Ponder the description in "Hildegard's Words" again. Have you ever met any prophets during your own life? If so, recall one of them and think about one of her or his gifts. What did this prophet teach you about yourself? About God? Offer a prayer of thanksgiving for the grace of being touched by her or him.

✧ Did you ever feel moved to speak out against injustice? Did you do it? Recall the circumstances of the event, and try to imagine what Hildegard would encourage you to do. Invite Hildegard into your imagination. Talk with her about your own call to be a prophetic voice.

✧ Read the following poem slowly and thoughtfully:

Dare to
declare
who you
are. It
isn't
far from
the shores
of silence
to the
boundaries
of speech.
The road
is not
long but
the way
is deep.
And you
must not
only
walk there,

you must
be prepared
to leap.

(Nicola Slee, "Conversations with Muse: You to Me,"
in "Women's Silence in Religious Education,"
British Journal of Religious Education, p. 32)

Does this poem tell you anything about overcoming your own timidity?

Choose a phrase from the poem and use it as a prayer during the rest of the day; for example, pray, "O God, help me be prepared to leap."

God's Word

There are many different gifts, but it is always the same Spirit; there are many different ways of serving, but it is always the same [God]. There are many different forms of activity, but in everybody it is the same God who is at work in them all. The particular manifestation of the Spirit granted to each one is to be used for the general good. To one is given from the Spirit the gift of utterance expressing wisdom; to another the gift of utterance expressing knowledge, in accordance with the same Spirit; . . . to another, prophecy. . . . But at work in all these is one and the same Spirit, distributing them at will to each individual. (1 Corinthians 12:4–11)

Closing prayer: Signing yourself with your thumb on your forehead, lips, and heart, pray these words:

May Christ be in my thoughts,
on my lips,
and in my heart.
Amen.

✧ Meditation 5 ✧

The Greening Power of Justice

Theme: The flourishing of justice brings a greening to the soul.

Opening prayer: In the spirit of Hildegard, I pray for a heart filled with justice.

About Hildegard

The word *justice* appears often on the pages of Hildegard's books and letters. In *Scivias*, she records a vision that she had of the tower of the church. One of the statues adorning the tower was that of Justice. Hildegard's description of the statue brilliantly illustrates her vision of justice:

> . . . [Justice] arises after Wisdom, and by the Holy Spirit works in all the justice of human beings. . . . She contains and keeps all the commandments God instituted for those who love her. . . . For she is greater than the human mind, and extends up into Heaven, just as she bent down from Heaven in the Incarnation of the Savior when He Who was the Son of God came forth from the Father, Who is true Justice. . . . She dwells in the purity of the minds of the just, who direct all their desire

toward obeying the justice of God, and so is as white as a cloud. And thus she prepares for herself a pleasant habitation in just hearts.

. . . Those human deeds that weigh people down do not cling to her, but only those that lead them to justification and life. For God is just; and she, fighting against the Devil, shows it in her exhortation . . . to the other virtues, which work for God. (Hart and Bishop, "*Scivias,*" p. 467)

To Hildegard, justice had to do with making right and making holy. In messianic times, prophets proclaimed that justice will flow like a river. This rich description suggests that justice brings new life in its path. Justice seeks to establish proper order in the world.

Hildegard was deeply aware of the lack of justice in the world in which she lived. In a letter to Prior Albert of Disibodenberg, she wrote of a voice that came to her in a vision and said: "O Justice, you are without a homeland; you are a foreigner in the city of those who make up fables. . . . They neither sigh for your mysteries nor for your friendship and yet you are Justice" (Fox, *Book of Divine Works*, p. 299). But in this same letter, Hildegard added that a new order could be accomplished, and so the work of justice should always be done in hope.

Pause: Ponder what justice means to you.

Hildegard's Words

And thus all who live justly in deeds of holiness love you with a true and perfect love; for you endow those who love you with all benefits and in the end you endow them with eternal life. Wisdom, however, pours into the chambers, that is, into the spirit of human beings, the justice of true faith through which alone God is known. There this faith presses out all the chill and dampness of vice in such a way that such things cannot germinate and grow again. At the same time faith presses out for itself all the powers of virtue in such a way that a noble wine can be poured into a goblet and offered to us as a beverage. On this account believers should rejoice and be glad in true faith in an eternal reward. They should bear before them the pennants of the good deeds they have accomplished. Thirsting for God's justice, they should now suckle the holy element from God's breast and never have enough of it, so that they will be forever refreshed by the vision of God. . . . When we grasp justice in this way, we shall surrender to it, taste virtue, and drink. We shall be strengthened by it . . . . In this way the just love God of whom they can never have too much but from whom they have bliss forever and ever. (Fox, *Book of Divine Works*, pp. 39–40)

Reflection

People who are passionately committed to the works of justice are nourished and energized by God, who is justice. For Hildegard, spirituality was communal, not simply a personal relationship with God. Christian spirituality focuses our relationships on other persons and on the nonhuman world. Our just actions nourish these relationships.

In Jewish theology, two activities embody spirituality: *devekut*, which means "clinging to God" or contemplation, and *tikkun o'lam*, which means "repair of the world" or the work of justice. "Clinging to God" and "repair of the world" are two sides of the same coin. Having an integrated spirituality without either element is impossible. Hildegard understood the need for this balance. Fascinated as she was with the structure and interdependence of all life, she saw the world as charged with God's glory and us human beings as entrusted with special responsibility for its well-being.

Hildegard's illuminations abound with the insight that a spirituality based upon relatedness involves not only a recognition of beauty and goodness but an openness to see tragedy and evil. Such openness allows the power of God's own resurrection in Jesus to effect the transforming good that God makes possible. Until the end of her life, Hildegard never lost

sight of the possibility of reformation and transformation because it was grounded in the hope that people could change
their heart and their ways.

✧ Pray repeatedly the lament "O Justice, you are without
a homeland." Then, ask yourself how justice has a place in
your heart and actions.

✧ Read again Hildegard's vision of justice in "About Hildegard." Ponder these statements and questions:
+ *"Justice arises after Wisdom."* What wisdom is required to do
   justice? What wisdom do you need to be more just?
+ *"The just . . . direct all their desire toward obeying the justice
   of God."* Can you say this for yourself? Where do you experience a desire for the justice of God?

✧ Read these words of a founder of monasticism, Saint
Basil the Great, who lived in the fourth century; ponder their
relevance for today's world and for your own life:

> The bread which you do not use
>   Is the bread of the hungry.
> The garment hanging in your wardrobe
>   Is the garment of one who is naked.
> The shoes that you do not wear
>   Are the shoes of one who is barefoot.
> The money you keep locked away
>   Is the money of the poor.
> The acts of charity you do not perform
>   Are so many injustices you commit.

✧ Who and what do you feel responsible for? What are
some concrete ways that you have recently shown your responsibility? Do Saint Basil's words suggest any other options
to you?

✧ Look around you and notice what is nearby. Try to
think of how you are related to as many of these objects as
possible: for example, the afghan that you made, the chair that
supports your body, the lamp that lights your eyes. Then, gaze
farther afield and do the same with whatever meets your

glance: for example, the sidewalk that guides your footsteps, the sun that warms your back, the air that fills your lungs, the flowers that delight your eye. Muse for a while at how wondrous God's creation is and what a blessed gift it is to be a partner with God in ministering to it.

✧ Can you do anything today to express your willingness to repair the world or to surrender to justice and good deeds?

✧ Thoughtfully read the following poem that describes how we might work to repair our bent, broken world:

> In the vacant places
> We will build with new bricks
> There are hands and machines
> And clay for new brick
> And lime for new mortar
> Where the bricks are fallen
> We will build with new stone
> Where the beams are rotten
> We will build with new timbers
> Where the word is unspoken
> We will build with new speech
> There is work together
> A Church for all
> And a job for each
> Every man [and woman] to [their] work.
> (T. S. Eliot, *The Complete Poems and Plays*, p. 98)

What is your "job" in building justice? Pray to the Holy Spirit for inspiration and courage.

God's Word

> Yahweh, you have favored your land
> and restored the well-being of Israel;
> you have forgiven the guilt of your people
> and covered all their sins.
>
> . . . .
> I will hear what you, God, proclaim:

a voice that speaks of peace—
peace for your faithful
and those who turn to you in hope.
Your salvation is near
for those who fear you,
and your glory will dwell in our land.
Love and faithfulness have met;
justice and peace have embraced.
Faithfulness shall spring from the earth
and justice look down from heaven.
Yahweh, you will give what is good,
and our earth shall yield its fruit.
Justice shall march before you,
and peace shall follow your steps.

(Psalm 85)

Closing prayer:

Praise to you
Spirit of fire!
· · · · · · · ·
Now gather us all to yourself
and in your mercy guide us
into the paths of justice.

(Newman, *"Symphonia,"* pp. 143, 147)

Amen.

✧ Meditation 6 ✧

The Beauty
of a Virtuous Life

Theme: Hildegard described the life of a good person as like an orchard filled with the fruit of good works.

Opening prayer: "I pray for the grace of an undivided heart, O my God, so that I can praise you with all my heart and proclaim your greatness forever by a virtuous life" (adapted from Psalm 86:11–12).

About Hildegard

Hildegard described a life of virtue as taking on the brilliant beauty of the stars. Virtue manifests itself through good works, which in themselves bring forth beauty. Hildegard also compared the beauty of a virtuous life to that of an orchard:

> Those of us who do good are like an orchard full of the fruit of good works. Such persons are like the Earth, which is strengthened and adorned by rocks and trees. But if we do evil works in the stubbornness of sin, we shall remain sterile in God's eyes, like the stubborn Earth that bears no fruit. (Fox, *Book of Divine Works*, p. 117)

In another vision, Hildegard pictured Beatitude this way:

Beatitude is the unconquered serenity of true glory, and fears no miseries in death. Therefore *she is clothed in a white tunic, picked out with green;* for she is surrounded by faithful works, which are bright with celestial desire and fresh with the freshness of the gifts of the Holy Spirit.

She has in her hands a small vase, pale and shining; . . . it gives off bright light like lightning, and this light shines on the face and neck of the figure. For knowledge of eternal light is diffused by both fear and love of God, which reaches from a person's inner heart to his face, which is to say it makes him begin righteous deeds that show his good intent. (Hart and Bishop, *"Scivias,"* p. 405; italics in original)

Pause: Ponder Hildegard's visions of virtue, and then reflect on this question: What does virtue mean to me?

Hildegard's Words

In good people, wisdom shows its own works of brightness. These works perfect and embellish the heavenly Jerusalem since they have already passed through the righteousness of justice. But where have these works come from? They come clearly from the height of heaven. As dew comes down from the clouds and covers the earth with its moisture, so also these good works come down from God and have been moistened for growing by the pouring over of the Holy Spirit. As a result, the faithful can produce good and sweet fruit, and they can obtain the heavenly Jerusalem. And so these good works, coming from heaven through the gifts of the Holy Spirit, have the brightness of the Spirit from whom they have flowed. What does this mean? The brightness of God shines in the good works of just people, so that God can be known, adored, and worshipped so lovingly on earth, and so that the virtues of these people can embellish the holy city with their decorations. For by doing good works with the help of God, people worship God with their countless and wonderful actions. (Bruce Hozeski, trans., *"Scivias," by Hildegard of Bingen*, p. 342)

Reflection

Living a virtuous life means cocreating with God's grace. God and the person cooperate to build the Reign of God. By believing and doing, the virtuous person grows strong. And throughout Hildegard's letters, books, and songs, the virtuous life always leads to beauty.

✧ Review the two readings in "About Hildegard" and "Hildegard's Words." Dwell on one line that seems to hold special meaning for you. Pray with this line, and allow God to speak through it. What is God saying to you?

✧ A wonderful form of prayer is guided meditation. In the following prayer, you are led to a quiet spot in an orchard, there to encounter Jesus:

Close your eyes. . . . Relax. . . . Let all the tension go. . . . Breathe deeply in and out . . . in and out. . . . Feel the tensions leave your feet. . . . If you need to, tense your muscles and then just let them relax . . . now your legs. . . . Relax your stomach and chest. . . . Now, let all the tensions escape from your arms . . . your neck. . . . Let your jaw and face relax, too. . . . Slow down . . . hear the breath of life flowing calmly in and out. . . .

Now, take a leisurely walk into an apple orchard. . . . The sun shines brightly overhead. . . . It's a perfect day, not too hot or too chill. . . . A soft breeze ruffles your hair. . . .

Slowly you walk down the rows of trees. . . . The apples sway gently overhead. . . . You marvel at tree after tree of fruit. . . .

In the middle of the apple grove, you meet a man who is checking on a tree that looks sickly. . . . He smiles at you, extends his hands, and says, "Peace be with you." . . . You recognize him as Jesus. . . . Taking his hands, you clasp them warmly. . . . Then, you sit together under an apple tree. . . .

Jesus points to the trees, saying, "Some bear McIntoshes, some Firesides, others Prairie Spys—and then some are sickly and bear little or nothing. . . . What fruit do you bear, my friend? Tell me about the beauty in your life. What are the good works that you do?" . . .

Taking a moment or two to ponder your answer, you soon begin telling Jesus of all the good that has come from God's grace to you. . . . You give him a complete accounting. . . .

When you finish, Jesus says, "You are known by your fruits. Be fruitful. Make of your life a beautiful orchard like this one. Good-bye, friend." . . . He walks away down the grove, checking trees for their yield and health. . . .

When you are ready, return from the scene and open your eyes.

After this guided meditation, you might wish to write any reactions in your journal.

✧ Pray that God makes you like a tree planted by the waterside, that you, too, may bear the fruit of good living.

✧ Picture a hillside with lovely vegetation—grass, shrubbery, and trees. The air is clean and fresh, perhaps because it is so near the Sea of Galilee. You are in the crowd that has been following Jesus to this place, and your heart is filled with expectation at what he might say. A hush comes over the people, and you hear these words:

How blessed are the poor in spirit:
. . . Heaven is theirs.
Blessed are the gentle:
they shall have the earth as inheritance.
Blessed are those who mourn:
they shall be comforted.
Blessed are those who hunger and thirst for uprightness:
they shall have their fill.
Blessed are the merciful:
they shall have mercy shown them.
Blessed are the pure in heart:
they shall see God.
Blessed are the peacemakers:
they shall be recognised as children of God.
Blessed are those who are persecuted in the cause of
uprightness:
. . . Heaven is theirs.

How blessed are the poor in spirit:
. . . Heaven is theirs.

(Matthew 5:3–10,3)

Ponder these images and words. Is one of these Beatitudes especially appealing to you? Carefully think about why this is so, and recall an instance or two in which you lived out the meaning of that Beatitude.

Is one Beatitude especially difficult for you? Consider why this might be so. Reflect on some possible ways to practice this Beatitude in your own life, and then choose one on which you can focus today or during the coming week. Slowly repeat the words of the Beatitude you have chosen as you bring your reflection to a close.

✧ Imagine another hillside—this one lush with green that sparkles with sunlight as it reflects the dew —in another time. This hill is on the bank of the Rhine and the year is 1138. Vineyards are planted in rows along the side of the hill, and farther up is the abbey where Hildegard and her sisters live. Picture some of the people who are making their way up the road as you travel alongside them. Notice how different they

are—young, old; rich, poor; learned, unlearned. Try to think of what they are going to visit Hildegard about. What will you ask Hildegard? Can you guess what she might tell you about the life you should lead?

God's Word

Beware of false prophets. . . . You will be able to tell them by their fruits. Can people pick grapes from thorns, or figs from thistles? In the same way, a sound tree produces good fruit but a rotten tree bad fruit. A sound tree cannot bear bad fruit, nor a rotten tree bear good fruit. Any tree that does not produce good fruit is cut down and thrown on the fire. I repeat, you will be able to tell them by their fruits. (Matthew 7:15–20)

Closing prayer:

Oh, the joys of those
. . . .
[who] delight in the law of Yahweh
and ponder it day and night.
They are like trees planted by streams of water
that yield fruit in due season,
whose leaves do not wither;
and everything they do prospers.

(Psalm 1:1–3)

Amen.

Wellness: The Call to Choose Life

Theme: God, our God, has blessed us with *viriditas*, or "the greening power of life," and desires that we nurture ourselves to wellness.

Opening prayer: I pray to you, God, the strength of my life, for gentle healing and fullness of life.

About Hildegard

Besides her mystical works, Hildegard wrote texts about nature and medicine. In Hildegard's day, Rupertsberg was famous as a drug dispensary. The monastery had a large herb garden. Several nuns worked in it, and Hildegard studied the plants and their curative powers there. She wrote of dietary prescriptions, gynecological cures, and what would today be recognized as homeopathic principles. Hildegard's medicine drew no clear distinctions between medical and miraculous ways of healing. All healing was fraught with mystery.

Hildegard made her beliefs about humanity clear when she declared the following:

Humankind along with every created thing, is the handiwork of God. But humankind is said to be also the worker of the Divinity, a reflection of the mysteries of God, and a revelation of the Holy Trinity. Indeed, God made them in his image and likeness. Just as Satan for all his malice, could not bring God to naught, so also he will not succeed in destroying the human race. (Silvas, "Saint Hildegard," *Tjurunga*, volume 31, p. 40)

In her written works on medicine and health, Hildegard showed a commonsense attitude in her observations of everyday life. For example, she compiled a list of thirty-five avoidable risk factors, such as stress and anger. Two modern commentators summarized Hildegard's conception of the relationship between our body and spirit this way:

> Weakness and loss of life-energy are the result of the tragedy of the loss of faith—the sin of allowing faith to dry out. A person who seems dried up has lost the power of creativity; the salvation from this desert, spiritual healing, comes as a gift of faith through Jesus Christ. (P. xxvii)
>
> Hildegard says that a harmonious interaction of all the bodily functions continually restores the organism's unimpeded function. The secretion of the hormonal glands, the function of the organs, the chemistry of the tissues and the body fluids, are all an intricate part of the total organism and influence our emotions and overall integrity, just as they affect our spirituality and vice-versa. (Dr. Wighard Strehlow and Gottfried Hertzka, *Hildegard of Bingen's Medicine*, p. 93)

Pause: Reflect on the splendor of the human being.

Hildegard's Words

According to Hildegard, wellness required moderation in all things:

> In a true vision I saw and heard the following words:
> *O daughter of God, out of your love for God you call a poor creature like myself, "Mother." Listen, then, to your mother and learn moderation! For moderation is the mother of all the*

virtues for everything heavenly and earthly. For it is through moderation that the body is nourished with the proper discipline. Any human being who thinks about her sins with sighs of regret—all those sins which she has committed in thought, word, and deed through the Devil's inspiration—must embrace this mother, discretion, and with the counsel of her religious superiors repent of her sins in true humility and sincere obedience. When there are unseasonable downpours, the fruit and vegetables growing on Earth are damaged; when a field has not been plowed, you do not find good grain springing up; instead, there are only useless weeds. It's the same with a person who lays on herself more strain than her body can endure. This is a sign that the effects of holy discretion are weak in such a person. And all of this immoderate straining and abstinence bring nothing useful to such a soul. (Fox, *Book of Divine Works*, pp. 340–341; italics in original)

Reflection

Very likely, Hildegard was often disturbed while writing and studying, for guests of all kinds came from other countries. Many of them were sick. Hildegard's door was open to all, but it was open farthest for those who bore sorrow and pain.

Hildegard saw suffering as it was—difficult to experience and hard to accept. She had plenty of practice in physical suffering herself. Though she thanked God for her illnesses, she did not enjoy the suffering. For her, suffering remained a burden that she lovingly accepted, but never desired—even as a sharing in the passion of Jesus.

Instead, wellness interested Hildegard. We know from her biographies that she had a sense of humor, a warm heart, balanced wisdom, and great joy in living. Though she did not practice medicine in the sense that we understand it today, Hildegard was a good doctor. She attended to healing body and soul.

✧ Marvel at the wondrousness of your body. You may wish to stand in front of a mirror as you affirm these parts of your being:

✦ your eyes, which admit such a palette of images from the outside and which are a mirror reflecting to the world your own inside

✦ your ears, which "are like two wings, which lead all the voices and tones in and out, just like wings carry the birds into the air" (Strehlow and Hertzka, *Medicine*, p. 11)

✦ your mouth, which is the instrument of speech

✦ your tongue, which admits delicious and varied tastes

Continue affirming and marveling at all the parts of your body.

✧ Write the story of your body. Begin with the first important event in your body's story and continue to the present. You might want to chronologically chart your story in three columns: in column 1, write down the year or years; in column 2, write a brief description of the important event (for example, having eye surgery, winning a bowling tournament); and in column 3, describe the physical, emotional, and spiritual effects you underwent at the time and over the long range (for example, if you had eye surgery, you may have experienced fear of blindness, sensitivity to the unsighted, self-consciousness, new appreciation for colors).

After describing the story of your body, select one point that is most important to you. Spend some time writing about why this event is most significant. How has this event shaped your attitude about your body and about yourself as a whole? Has your body's story influenced the ways in which you have related to God? Dialog with God about this question.

✧ If possible, find family portraits from your childhood, adolescence, and young adulthood. If you cannot find a picture, close your eyes and compose a picture of your immediate family in your imagination.

Study the picture or pictures. Were members of your family pleased with the body God gave them? Who liked his or her body and who did not seem to? Try to remember particular examples for each person that demonstrated their liking or disliking their body.

Of the members of your family, who was most influential in the formation of your attitudes about your body? Was what you learned from this person about your body mostly positive or negative? Are you still holding on to what this person taught you?

Imagine that you are talking to this person, with Jesus or Hildegard present during the conversation. Tell the person about how she or he hurt or helped your body image. Do not hold anything back. Then, imagine this person's responses. Listen carefully. Finally, let Jesus or Hildegard talk to both of you. What does Jesus or Hildegard say to heal or support you?

✧ Reflect on how your inside affects your outside; that is, how stress and anxiety, or happiness and contentment, affect your physical well-being.

✧ Should you apologize to your body for anything—for example, overwork, not enough sleep, poor eating habits?

Ask your body and God for forgiveness. Resolve to be more attentive to your body.

✧ Consider what you regularly do to nourish your spirit. Think about how much of a priority this "soul food" is to you.

✧ Do you feel that Hildegard might urge you to make some changes in the way you treat your body and nourish your soul? If so, what might they be? How might your life be different if you were to make these changes?

✧ Complete your reflection by just dwelling a few moments on the rapture of being alive.

God's Word

Do you not realise that your body is the temple of the Holy Spirit, who is in you and whom you received from God? You are not your own property, then; you have been bought at a price. So use your body for the glory of God. (1 Corinthians 6:19–20)

Closing prayer: "My God, you constantly restore my life. Help me to remember that I hold this treasure in a fragile pot of earthenware. May I never forget that your life is at work in me. And grant me the strength to always choose life. Amen" (adapted from 2 Corinthians 4:7,12).

✧ Meditation 8 ✧

God's Wondrous Works

Theme: Hildegard loved creation, and she believed that one of the best ways to know God was to love God's works of art.

Opening prayer: How tremendous are your deeds, O God. All the earth worships you and sings praise to you. I pray to be able always to wonder at what you have done.

About Hildegard

Bishop Eberhard II of Bamberg wrote to Hildegard, asking her to explain how eternity lived in God, how equality lived in Jesus, and how the Holy Spirit unified eternity and equality. Hildegard's answering letter contained a long explanation, but one part of it manifested her beliefs about the wonders of creation:

> The Father is brightness and this brightness has a flashing forth and in this flashing forth is fire and these three are one. Whoever doesn't hold fast to this in faith doesn't gaze on God, because he or she wants to separate from God that which is. For no one should divide God. Even the works God has made disappear when someone conceptually divides them up, splitting up the full content of these names. The brightness is therefore the fatherhood

from which all things come and which surrounds everything. For all things live from its power.

The same power also formed the first human being and communicated to him the breath of life. It is thus from this power that human beings have the ability to be active in the world. In what way? Flesh proceeds from flesh; goodness—whatever is of good reputation—proceeds from what is good and it is increased through the good example of other people. This takes place bodily and spiritually in human beings, for the one proceeds from the other as the other. Human beings love the things they make because from their recognition they see that they gain reality. God wants the same thing. God wants the divine power to be manifested in all created forms because they are divine works. (Fox, *Book of Divine Works*, pp. 277–278)

Pause: Ask yourself: Have I ever tried to separate the glory of God from God's creation?

Hildegard's Words

God's throne is, indeed, the divine eternity in which God alone abides, and all living creatures are, so to speak, sparks from the radiation of God's brilliance, and these sparks emerge from God like the rays of the sun. And how would God be known as life if not through the fact that the realm of the living, which glorifies and praises God also emerges from God? On this account God has established the living, burning sparks as a sign of the brilliance of God's renown. All creatures should see that God has neither beginning nor end, and for this reason they will never have enough of looking at God. Thus they will behold God eagerly and without satiety, and their eagerness will never slacken. How would the One who alone is eternal be known if not so regarded by the angels? But if God did not give off those sparks, how would the divine glory become fully visible? And how would God be known as the Eternal One if brilliance did not emerge from God? For there is no creature without some kind of radiance—whether it be greenness, seeds, buds, or another kind of beauty. Otherwise, it would not be a creature at all. But if God did not have the power to make all things, where would God's creative power be? (Fox, *Book of Divine Works*, pp. 86–87)

Reflection

Hildegard believed that God was delighted with creation, and her conviction was reflected in her lifeworks. Curious about many things and wonder-filled at the beauty of creation, she wrote on a grand scale. She focused on the cosmic implications of the Creation, the Fall, the Redemption, and the Last Judgment of the world. The emphasis in her writings was on the order and structure of the universe in all its magnificence and splendor, and the mystery revealed in the ever-unfolding drama of its history.

She believed that whatever God created was bound together in cosmic interdependence. Even though sin flawed the universe, Hildegard nonetheless marveled at human excellence and praised a suffering and struggling humanity as God's supreme achievement. In Hildegard's view, we human beings are essentially rational beings, and through our intelligence we are most closely united to the divine. Intelligence—that is, reason informed by feeling and feeling informed by reason—is God's greatest gift to us. Through the intellect and the imagination that it inspires, we can be shown the way to everlasting splendor.

According to Hildegard, life, the world, and God are far from boring. God is full of immeasurable glory and abundant sweetness, which are reflected in creation.

✦ Slowly reread the passage in "Hildegard's Words," and choose a phrase that is especially provocative for you. Repeat it several times now and then throughout the day.

✦ Imagine or, better still, visit a place that is filled with God's marvelous works: perhaps a park, garden, field, or hillside. Observe every creation present there, feeling the wonder it brings to you. Before you leave it, consider ways you might share this place and your feelings about it with someone else, and then offer God thanksgiving and praise for this scene in silent prayer or with a song.

✧ Have you ever felt bored with life? Was it like being one of the following?
+ stuck
+ listless
+ indifferent
+ withdrawn
You might wish to add your own words to describe the feeling of boredom you experienced. Recall what it took for you to lose that feeling.

✧ Contrast your experience of boredom with the joy of living that you have known at other times. You may wish to focus on one occasion in which you felt especially aware of relishing life. Record the joyous time in your journal. After a time for cherishing this memory, thank God for your ability to savor life.

✧ Hildegard marveled at the human intellect—our ability to reason and to imagine. List several times today when you had to gather data, think through a problem logically, and make a decision. Then, list several instances when you imagined possibilities, pleasant scenes, or past events. Discuss with God the gift of your intellect.

✧ Meditatively read the following poem by e. e. cummings, and muse for a while on any similarities you find between Hildegard's words and his point of view:

i thank You God for most this amazing
day: for the leaping greenly spirits of trees
and a blue true dream of sky; and for everything
which is natural which is infinite which is yes

(i who have died am alive again today,
and this is the sun's birthday; this is the birth
day of life and of love and wings: and of the gay
great happening illimitably earth)

how should tasting touching hearing seeing
breathing any—lifted from the no
of all nothing—human merely being
doubt unimaginable You?

(now the ears of my ears awake and
now the eyes of my eyes are opened)

(*One Hundred Selected Poems*, p. 95)

God's Word

Alleluia!
I will thank you, Yahweh, with all my heart

· ·
Great are your works
to be pondered by all who love them.
Glorious and sublime are your works;
your justice stands firm forever.
You help us remember your wonders.
You are compassion and love.

(Psalm 111:1–4)

Closing prayer: Alleluia! I celebrate you, my God; and I give you thanks, for your love is everlasting. I pray that I may never take your love for granted, nor fail to recognize your marvelous works all about me.

Caring for the Earth

Theme: Hildegard understood that for those who live in Christ, all creation is God's work, and that the earth especially is waiting with eagerness to be saved.

Opening prayer: I pray for the grace to cherish the earth and to always marvel at the glory of God's creation.

About Hildegard

When she was about sixty-five years old, Hildegard saw a marvelous vision. Through this vision she understood that love established the pillars that hold up the earth and that people—created in God's own image and likeness—share in God's work: they are cocreators. The power of the earth to reveal God's love stunned Hildegard. She believed that all creation sings to and worships God.

In a letter to Bishop Eberhard II of Bamberg, Hildegard declared:

> And it is written: "The Spirit of the Lord fills the Earth." This means that no creature, whether visible or invisible, lacks a spiritual life. . . . The clouds too have their course to run. The moon and stars flame in fire. The trees shoot forth buds because of the power in their seeds. Water has a delicacy and a lightness of motion like the wind.

This is why it springs up from the Earth and pours itself into running brooks. Even the Earth has moisture and mist.

All creatures have something visible and invisible. (P. 281)

. . . No tree blossoms without greening power; no stone is without moisture; no creature is without its own power. (Fox, *Book of Divine Works*, p. 277)

Hildegard held the earth as precious. Caring for the living and delicate earth became a sacred trust for her.

As the bearer of secrets waiting to be shared and surprises yearning to be discovered, the earth provided a workplace for Hildegard well into her old age. Indeed, near the end of her life, she told Gottfried of Saint Disibod and Dieter of Echternach, two of her brother monks and earliest biographers, that when she had the splendid vision of the earth held up on pillars of love, all her "inner parts trembled" and the image brought on one of her rare ecstasies (Silvas, "Saint Hildegard," *Tjurunga*, volume 31, p. 39). The earth became the stuff of her most intense religious experience.

Later in her talks with Gottfried and Dieter, Hildegard declared that God's presence is manifest through the gorgeous works of creation. Creation reveals the hidden God just as clothes hint at the shape of a person's body.

Pause: Reflect on the sheer beauty of the earth.

Hildegard's Words

Hildegard recorded these words, spoken by God to her in a vision:

I am the supreme and fiery force who kindled every living spark, and I breathed forth no deadly thing—yet I permit them to be. As I circle the whirling sphere with my upper wings (that is, with wisdom), rightly I ordained it. And I am the fiery life of the essence of God: I flame above the beauty of the fields; I shine in the waters; I burn in the sun, the moon, and the stars. And, with the airy wind, I quicken all things vitally by an unseen, all-sustaining life. For the air is alive in the verdure and the flowers; the waters flow as if they lived; the sun too lives in its light; and when the moon wanes it is rekindled by the light of the sun, as if it lived anew. Even the stars glisten in their light as if alive. . . .

I flame above the beauty of the fields to signify the earth—the matter from which God made man. I shine in the waters to indicate the soul, for, as water suffuses the whole earth, the soul pervades the whole body. I burn in the sun and the moon to denote reason, and the stars are the innumerable words of reason. (Newman, *Sister of Wisdom,* pp. 69–70)

Reflection

Hildegard celebrated the sacramental character of the universe. God flames in the fields, shines in the waters, and suffuses the whole earth.

However, Mother Earth is in terrible trouble today, considering such ecological disasters as the depletion of the ozone layer, the destruction of the rain forests, massive oil spills in the water, and the contamination of the soil. Awareness is growing that these patterns of abuse must change. The world's environment must be healed and the rape of the earth stopped before the damage becomes irreparable. We will all bear the consequences if we neglect our Mother Earth. The words of the prophet Isaiah ring all too true:

The earth is mourning, pining away,

. . . .
The earth is defiled
by the feet of its inhabitants,
for they have transgressed the laws,
violated the decree, broken the everlasting covenant.

(24:4–5)

The ecosystem's disaster symbolizes a lack of care and reverence for all living things. The rape of the environment provides a mirror image of violence people use to control and dominate each other. In the biblical injunction to have dominion over the earth, the word *dominion* originally meant "care."

If we were to regard Mother Earth as a living body that is also our home, perhaps it would be easier to see ourselves as partners with her. Hildegard's keen sense of divine imminence can help us to understand that God's creative power enfolds the earth and energizes it from within. Recognizing God's presence in all of creation can also help us to recognize our responsibility to cherish the earth and to care for it.

✧ Read the revelation in "Hildegard's Words" again. Ponder each line's meaning for you. Spend extra time praying one line that says most to you. Use this line today as the focus of your prayer, during spare moments or while you are waiting.

✧ Meditate on the earth. Take the long view and the short view. Start by picturing the earth from the perspective of a space capsule orbiting it. Notice the masses of soil and water on this swirling planet that we call home. Notice also that no other boundaries are visible at this distance. Imagine the earth's neighbors that fill the universe—the clusters of stars, the sun and moon, the other planets—and see how they all fit in the vast space.

After a while, look at the earth from where you sit. How much can you see? What do you notice? Is the sky visible? Are trees or flowers within eyesight? Is litter strewn about or any other sign of pollution present? How does this make you feel?

✧ If possible, go outdoors and touch the earth. You may wish to kneel down or sit down so that you can place your hands on it for a few moments. Let your sense of touch speak to you. What are some of the things you notice? Talk with God or Hildegard about your feelings and thoughts.

✧ Fill a bowl with some soil and bring it indoors. Keep it at your prayer space for a few days. Let it serve as a gentle reminder of the care that all the earth deserves. Perhaps you can tenderly finger the soil for a few moments before beginning your daily prayer.

✧ Remember some of the happy moments you had with the earth when you were young: for instance, playing in the sand, wading in the water, hiking with friends, picnicking on a blanket outdoors, lying on your back and watching the clouds. Whisper a prayer of thanksgiving for the gift of Mother Earth.

✧ Do an examen of consciousness about how you care for Mother Earth. Here are some questions with which to begin your examen:

✦ Am I committed to recycling any object that can be used again, including metals, glass, plastic, paper, clothing, and so on?

✦ Do I use appliances and vehicles that depend on natural resources conscientiously? Air conditioner? Stove? Lights? Automobile?

✦ Do I use any harmful chemicals? Aerosols? Styrofoam? Pesticides?

✦ Do I garden, exercise, eat healthy foods, plant trees, walk, bicycle, and do other activities that are healthy for me and for the planet?

✦ Do I support individuals and organizations committed to protecting the earth from harm and nurturing ravaged parts of it back to health?

✧ Do something now or as soon as possible to touch and care for the earth. Go out for a brisk walk. Hike through a forest preserve. Prepare a pot or plot and plant some flowers. Start a compost heap. Get your car tuned up and organize a car pool.

God's Word

O God, our Savior—
. . . .
By your power you hold the mountains firm,
you who are armed with might.
You calm the roaring of the seas,
the roaring of their waves
and the tumult among nations.
Those who live at the ends of the earth
are in awe at your marvels;
you make east and west resound with joy.
You have cared for the land and watered it;
greatly you have enriched it.
God's streams are filled;
you have provided the grain.
Thus have you prepared the land:
drenching its furrows,
breaking up its clods,
softening it with showers,
blessing its yield.

(Psalm 65:5–10)

Closing prayer: O God, may I never forget how precious is the earth to you. Help me to cherish every bit of the earth so that in doing so, I will be reminded of you who created and sustains this garden of delights, which I call home. And may the care I show for it be a reflection of my love for all living things.

> O limpid mirror of God . . .
>
> Out of you clouds
> come streaming, winds
> take wing from you, dashing
> rain against stone;
> and ever-fresh springs
> well from you, washing
> the evergreen globe.

> (Newman, *"Symphonia,"* pp. 149, 151)

Amen. Alleluia!

✧ Meditation 10 ✧

The Lovely Voice of Compassion

Theme: For Hildegard, the compassion of the human community for poor people reflects God's own compassion for the world. To be compassionate is to be God-like.

Opening prayer: I pray to you with Hildegard's words, "O Living Fountain, how great is Your sweet compassion!" (Hart and Bishop, "*Scivias,*" p. 529).

About Hildegard

Hildegard was a prophetess and mystic, but she also practiced medicine. Consistent with the Benedictines' tradition of hospitality, her abbey ministered to visitors, especially to sick people who came for treatment. Like every truly holy person, Hildegard was moved into action by her charity or compassion.

Five abbots from Burgundy wrote Hildegard, asking her to pray for a noble couple whose child had died and who were unable to have more children. Responding, Hildegard described compassion in warm imagery:

Live with clear simplicity in the clefts of the walls, so that you can sing songs of praise and salvation in the tents of the just. For God has sunk deep in our reason the lively, bursting sound of the breath of life—namely, the sound of rejoicing, that through the knowledge of the good sees and recognizes God in faith. This sound reverberates in all the works of good will like the full-toned notes of a trumpet. It carries in itself an all-embracing love, so that it is also able through humility to gather around itself the gentle and thorough compassion to be a balm to every wound.

Love streams down with the outpouring water of the Holy Spirit, and in this love is the peace of God's goodness. And humility prepares a garden with all the fruit-bearing trees of God's grace, containing all the green of God's gifts. Compassion, on the other hand, drips balsam for all the needs that adhere to the human condition. This sound of love rings in harmony with every hymn of thanks for salvation. Through humility it sounds in the heights where love beholds God and victoriously battles against pride. This love calls out in compassion with a pleading yet lovely voice. It gathers the poor and the lame around itself and begs so intensely for the help of the Holy Spirit that this same love is able to bring everything to fulfillment through good works. Love sounds in the tents where the saints shine on the thrones they have built for themselves in this world. (Fox, *Book of Divine Works*, pp. 313–314)

Pause: Ponder the meaning of compassion for you.

Hildegard's Words

In the eighth vision that Hildegard recorded in *Scivias,* she described the figure of Charity this way:

The true and ardent lamp of Charity was lighted when God so loved humanity that for its love He sent His Only-Begotten to take a human body. . . . And so He inflamed them [humankind] with Charity that they might faithfully assist all the needy, and this virtue is clothed with the tunic of God's sweetness that she may shine upon all people with true light for their devotion, use and profit.

You shall therefore do these things with all your heart, and all your soul, and all your strength, and all your mind, that nothing may be wanting to you in faith. . . . You shall also love yourself. How? If you love God, you love your salvation. And, loving yourself in all this, you shall also love your neighbor. . . . You shall rejoice in his righteous prosperity and heavenly salvation. (Hart and Bishop, "Scivias," pp. 442–443)

Reflection

The word *compassion* means "to suffer with." So, compassionate persons are those who recognize their part in the suffering human condition. When we become aware of our common identity, we can be moved to "feel" with others and to "be" with others in their painful place.

Hildegard was a passionate woman who understood that care for others should not be meted out in predetermined amounts. Compassion takes shape in generous and cheerful action. One form of compassion is the sharing of material wealth. This sharing adds a public and a physical dimension to compassion.

The fruit of charity or compassion is the affirmation of our own humanity and the humanity of the persons to whom we minister. Compassion helps us know and experience God.

✧ Take your time. Read "About Hildegard" once more. Write your reflections on what the quoted passage means for you. Slowly pray one line from the reading.

✧ Try to think of some images for people of compassion. For example, a compassionate person may be like the following:
✦ a cup filled to the brim and running over
✦ a well that does not run dry
✦ an eagle that bears me up on its wings

✧ Visit someone who is homebound, ill, or grieving. Consider how you might make such visits a regular part of your spirituality.

✧ How can you feed the hungry? Could any shelters for homeless people use your help? Can you build into your practice of compassion contributions to food banks?

✧ Write a list of ways in which you do or can act compassionately in your place of work. Pray for the resolve to act more compassionately to co-workers, customers, employers, and so on.

✧ Recall an instance in which someone was especially compassionate to you. Bring to mind the circumstances of that occasion, and then offer a prayer of thanksgiving to God for the person who gave you the gift of his or her compassion.

✧ Do you now feel compassionate toward anyone? Imagine yourself talking with that person. What might you say and do to convey your solidarity with her or him? Could you do anything today for her or him?

God's Word

God's spirit dwells within me, for I have been anointed by God. I am being sent to spread good tidings to the people who suffer, are sick at heart, and are languishing in captivity. This is the year of God's blessings. Mourning should cease. I will bestow wreaths of flowers to replace their ashes and change depression to happiness. (Adapted from Isaiah 61:1–3)

Closing prayer:

O Eternal Vigor,
all of creation is arranged and in order in your very heart.
Through your Word, all things are created just as you wish.
Your very own word even took on flesh in the same form
    that derived from Adam,

and thus removes heart-breaking pain from that very
   garment humanity wears.

O how magnificent is the compassion of the Saving One,
who frees all things by his becoming one with human life.
Divinity breathes into compassion without the chains of sin,
And so removes heart-breaking pain from that very
   garment humanity wears.

Glory to the Father and to the Son and to the Holy Spirit.
And so removes heart-breaking pain from that very
   garment humanity wears.

(Fox, Book of Divine Works, p. 384)

Beauty
and the Spiritual Life

Theme: The human heart hungers for beauty. Hildegard's life and works expressed this need, and they were filled with examples teaching us that beauty reveals the harmony of all things, the harmony that is truth.

Opening prayer: I pray for the grace to *see* the beautiful and to *make* beauty in my everyday life.

About Hildegard

The visions Hildegard received from God came as vivid images or pictures. First, she wrote down a description of an image and its meaning, and then later, she had each image painted in miniatures. Each of these visions was eventually illuminated at great cost in rich colors and gold and silver leaf. Because of their unique style and close correspondence to Hildegard's visions, it is thought that the illuminations were probably supervised by Hildegard. She wanted the beauty of the paintings to reflect the beauty and grandeur of her experience of God. Tragically, the only original copy of the illuminations disappeared with the bombing of Dresden during World War II. A photocopy survived, and from it, artists have reconstructed versions of the originals.

The illuminations allowed Hildegard to present a vision of wholeness at a time when the world of religion and politics had no clear sense of direction. They were wonderful gifts of visual music that celebrate the human imagination. The energy of Hildegard's own spirituality comes through to us in the rich symbolism employed: trees, water, flowers, fire, wings, sun, and vibrant colors.

Hildegard respected the role that our senses play in nourishing our soul. Art and all beauty touch the senses and, thence, the spirit. In turn, our senses express the condition of our soul. Commenting on the senses, Hildegard said:

> It is the senses on which the interior powers of the soul depend, so that these powers are known through them by the fruits of each work. . . . The exterior human being awakens with senses in the womb of his mother before he is born, but the other powers of the soul still remain in hiding. What is this? The dawn announces the daylight; just so the human senses manifest the reason and all the powers of the soul. And so on the two commandments of God hang all the Law and the prophets, so also on the soul and its powers depend the human senses. . . .
>
> . . . Human senses protect a person from harmful things and lay bare the soul's interior. For the soul emanates the senses. How? It vivifies a person's face and glorifies him with sight, hearing, taste, smell and touch, so that by this touch he becomes watchful in all things. For the senses are the sign of all the powers of the soul, as the body is the vessel of the soul. What does this mean? A person is recognized by his face, sees with his eyes, hears with his ears, opens his mouth to speak, feels with his hands, walks with his feet; and so the senses are to a person as precious stones and as a rich treasure sealed in a vase. But as the treasure within is known when the vase is seen, so also the powers of the soul are inferred by the senses. (Hart and Bishop, "Scivias," p. 123)

Jesus, the exemplar-artist, used ordinary language to describe eternal truths; so too did Hildegard in her writings. More important, Jesus showed us that human life can be a work of art far exceeding any masterpiece in its beauty. Human beings are icons of God—that is, sensory images that have shape, color, measure, and volume. Human life, as well as works of art like the illuminations, manifests God's greatness and beauty.

Pause: Recall a work of art, a piece of writing, or some natural object that has touched your soul.

Hildegard's Words

We are dressed in the scaffold of creation:
      in seeing—to recognize all the world,
      in hearing—to understand,
      in smelling—to discern,
      in tasting—to nurture,
      in touching—to govern.
In this way humankind comes to know God,
for God is the author of all creation.

And so,
humankind
full of creative possibilities,
is God's work.

Humankind alone,
is called to assist God.

Humankind is called to co-create.

God gave to humankind the talent
to create with all the world.

Just as the [people] shall never end,
until into dust they are transformed and resurrected,
just so,
their works are always visible.

The good deeds shall glorify,
the bad deeds shall shame,
insofar as they have not been blotted out through penance.

(Uhlein, *Meditations*, pp. 104, 106, 125)

Reflection

Hildegard knew that art enriches the imagination. It stirs our heart. It makes cold hearts warm and dry spirits moist again.

Hildegard also taught that art can influence spirituality because a work that is formed by the Spirit actually communicates the Spirit. Perhaps that is why Hildegard's illuminations are so compelling: they show us the goal toward which the life of the Spirit destines us—that is, transformation in Jesus Christ.

When we express our spirituality through art—by drawing, painting, sculpting, fashioning pictures with words or music, or making beautiful things such as embroidery, knit goods, woven fabrics—we ground our spirituality in creation. The careful making of beautiful things helps us to center ourselves so that we become still and filled with reverence for the stuff with which we work. Created works also manifest the energy toward the good with which the Creator has gifted us.

✧ Read again the passage about the senses in "About Hildegard." Then, sitting comfortably, close your eyes. Breathe deeply and slowly. Listen to each sound. Smell all there is to smell. Rub your hands over your clothes, your hair, the sides of the chair. Next, open your eyes; observe objects in the room. Study each object in detail, noticing its design, function, and overlooked beauty. Thank God for the ordinary use of your senses and how they can open you to beauty.

✧ Pause to notice all the things of beauty around you. If it is helpful, walk around, pick up objects, feel their textures. Note the work of human hands and heart that went into each object. Think, when was the last time you made a thing of beauty? How did it make you feel?

✧ Art also teaches us about mystery. Read these lines written by Richard Wilbur:

All that we do
Is touched with ocean, yet we remain
On the shore of what we know.
("For Dudley," in *Walking to Sleep*, p. 24)

This is the universal human condition, to live on the edge of mystery. To penetrate that mystery, we must learn from those who have gone further in the exploration of the ocean—that is, from those whose creative imagination is more powerful than our own, as in artists who render beautiful works. From whom have you learned about exploring the ocean of mystery? Thank God for the gift of this person's presence in your life and for his or her ability to lure you to probe life more deeply.

✧ Reflect on gifts you have that you can use more frequently in your work. What gifts do you want to use? What gifts do you wish to nurture more?

✧ Read these lines from the song "Bread and Roses" by Mimi Farina and J. Oppenheim:

Hearts starve as well as bodies;
give us bread but give us roses.

What do these words mean to you? Do you have bread, but no roses? Is your heart starving? Half-full? What might you do to feed your heart and give yourself and other people roses?

God's Word

We are God's work of art, created in Christ Jesus for the good works which God has already designated to make up our way of life. (Ephesians 2:10)

Closing prayer: I pray for the grace to recognize God's gifts to me in the work of creation. I pray, too, for the inspiration to imagine how I might make their beauty real in my own life and the life of others. May my works bear fruit that will last. May I make my life a work of God's art. Amen.

✧ Meditation 12 ✧

The Melody of Spirituality

Theme: Wherever there is Godlife, there too is music.

Opening prayer:

> O Yahweh, it is good to give you thanks,
> to sing psalms to your name, O Most High;
> to declare your love in the morning
> and your faithfulness every night,
> with the music of a ten-stringed lute,
> to the melody of the harp.
>
> (Psalm 92:1–3)

About Hildegard

Music was for Hildegard the highest form of praise. In her memoirs, Hildegard recalled how she came to compose music. She said: "I also brought forth and chanted hymns, with their melodies praising God and his saints, although here too, I had never studied neums or any chant notation at all." One of her biographers wrote that after Hildegard's visions, "who would not marvel at that harmonious music of a most sweet and wonderful melody that she composed . . . ?" (Silvas, "Life," *Tjurunga*, volume 30, pp. 70, 68).

In a report about Hildegard that her sisters wrote after her death, Hedwig of Alzey mentioned how eagerly Hildegard sang. She went singing through the cloisters or the garden accompanied by her nuns. For her, music was the embodiment of joy.

Hildegard's versatility and talent as a poet and composer show in the many songs she wrote. Yet, the greatest source of joy for Hildegard and her nuns was the Divine Office with its hymns and psalms. In a letter to the prelates of Mainz, Hildegard described the importance of singing and music:

> So remember: just as the body of Jesus Christ was born by the Holy Spirit from the spotless Virgin Mary, so too the singing in the Church of God's praise, which is an echo of the harmony of heaven, has its roots in that same Holy Spirit. But the body is the garment of the soul and it is the soul which gives life to the voice. That's why the body must raise its voice in harmony with the soul for the praise of God. . . . God should be praised with crashing cymbals, with cymbals of clear praise and with all the other musical instruments that clever and industrious people have produced. For all the arts serving human desires and needs are derived from the breath that God sent into the human body. And that is why it is fitting that God be praised in all. (Fox, *Book of Divine Works*, pp. 358–359)

Divine music came through the inspiration of the Holy Spirit. And Hildegard took this belief even further. In her "Symphony of Mary," she praised Mary as bearing not only the Word but the Song of God in her flesh:

> Your womb held joy when all heaven's
> harmony rang from you,
> for virgin, you bore the Son of God
> when in God your chastity blazed.
>
> . . . .
> Let the whole Church flush with rapture
> and resound with song
> for the sake of sweet Mary,
> the maiden all-praised,
> the Mother of God.
>
> (Newman, *Sister of Wisdom*, p. 180)

For Hildegard, the Incarnation brings musical harmony back into creation. Jesus is a song of praise and celebration.

Pause: Reflect on the power of music to light up your spirit.

Hildegard's Words

The song of rejoicing softens hard hearts, and draws forth from them the tears of compunction, and invokes the Holy Spirit. And so *those voices you hear are like the voice of a multitude, which lifts its sound on high;* for jubilant praises, offered in simple harmony and charity, lead the faithful to that consonance in which is no discord. . . .

Therefore, let everyone who understands God by faith faithfully offer [God] tireless praises, and with joyful devotion sing to [God] without ceasing. (Hart and Bishop, "*Scivias*," p. 534; italics in original)

To the Trinity be praise!
God is music, God is life
that nurtures every creature in its kind.
Our God is the song of the angel throng
and the splendor of secret ways
hid from all humankind,
But God our life is the life of all.
(Newman, "*Symphonia*," p. 143)

Reflection

Hildegard's life of passionate creativity bubbled over into her music, and her songs were so intensely motivated by her devotional life that they become an embodiment of her spirituality. Her songs combined rich poetry and a wondrous range of intricately simple melodies. The words of her liturgical songs symbolized the humanity of Christ, and the vibrant music indicated the Spirit.

In medieval times, the singing of plainchant was a central spiritual exercise. The meaning of the words was to be internalized, digested, and then released through the voice. The more focused and attentive were the singers to the words, the more powerfully was the inner meaning of the text revealed to the listeners and the singers themselves. Singing was indeed praying for Hildegard, and beautiful music was meditation and revelation. Not simply a frill, music pleased both rich and poor people because it touched their common humanity.

✧ Reread the words to "Symphony of Mary" in "About Hildegard." Let your imagination bathe in the images.

✧ Imagine the sound of music to be like perfume whose fragrance rises to fill the air with its sweetness. Is a piece of music especially pleasing to you because of its power to lift up your soul? Play a recording of it if you have it handy. Better yet, hum the melody or sing the words, and let the feelings they evoke run through you.

✧ In Hildegard's liturgical drama called *Ordo Virtutum*, all the parts are set to music except that of the Devil. Because the Devil is the spirit opposed to all harmony, the Devil is incapable of song. Evil is cacophony; good is harmony. Is anything in your life in discord? What would it take to bring harmony back? Converse with Jesus or Hildegard about this.

✧ Recall a favorite hymn—one that you enjoy singing in church. Sing the hymn. Ponder why this particular sacred song is so meaningful to you. You might wish to recall this hymn throughout the day and hum its melody as a prayer.

God's Word

My heart is ready, O God;
I will sing, sing your praise
and make music with all my soul.
Awake, lyre and harp.
I will wake the dawn.
I will praise you, Yahweh, among the peoples;
among the nations I will give thanks,
for your love reaches to the heavens
and your faithfulness to the skies.
O God, arise above the heavens;
may your glory be over the earth!

(Psalm 108:1–5)

Closing prayer: O God, I will sing and make melody to you as best I can. Do not consider the greatness of my voice or the skill of my playing, but rather the love in my heart.

✧ Meditation 13 ✧

Mary

Theme: Hildegard's devotion to Mary was distinctive and constant.

Opening prayer: I greet you and pray to you, Mary, in the words of Hildegard:

O loveliest and most loving Mother, hail!
You have given forth into this world your Son,
sent from heaven and breathed into you by the Spirit
    of God.
Praised be the Father, the Son, and Holy Spirit.
Breathed into you by the Holy Spirit.
(Fox, Book of Divine Works, p. 371)

About Hildegard

Of all her many works, Hildegard's hymns teach us the most about her distinctive devotion to Mary. Unlike many of her contemporaries, Hildegard ignored inauthentic legends about Mary's birth and childhood, and she did not display devotion to sentimental images of Mary nursing her child or weeping for him at the foot of the cross.

To Hildegard, the pre-eminent image of Mary was mother of Jesus. Through Mary, Jesus became flesh to show the human face of God. All of human history, according to Hildegard, pointed to the Incarnation. Mary's courage, faith, and love helped bring about this most important event. One of Hildegard's greatest compositions is this song to Mary, mother of Jesus:

De Sancta Maria (*To Mary*)

Hail to you, O greenest, most fertile branch!
You budded forth amidst breezes and winds
in search of the knowledge of all that is holy.
When the time was ripe
your own branch brought forth blossoms.
Hail, greetings to you!
The heat of the sun exudes sweat from you
like the balsam's perfume.
In you, the most stunning flower has blossomed
and gives off its sweet odor to all the herbs and roots,
which were dry and thirsting before your arrival.
Now they spring forth in fullest green!
Because of you, the heavens give dew to the grass,
the whole Earth rejoices;
Abundance of grain comes from Earth's womb
and on its stalk and branches the birds nest.
And, because of you, nourishment is given to the human
    family
and great rejoicing to those who gathered round the table.
And so, in you O gentle Virgin,
is every fullness of joy, everything that Eve rejected.
Now let endless praise resound to the Most High!
               (Fox, *Book of Divine Works*, p. 379)

Pause: Marvel at how much God loves humanity in that God chose one of us, Mary, to bring forth Jesus, the light of the world.

Hildegard's Words

In a vision, Hildegard experienced Mary this way:

> *And on her breast shines a red glow like the dawn;* for the virginity of the Most Blessed Virgin when she brought forth the Son of God glows with the most ardent devotion in the hearts of the faithful. *And you hear a sound of all kinds of music singing about her, "Like the dawn, greatly sparkling";* for, as you are now given to understand, all believers should join with their whole wills in celebrating the virginity of that spotless Virgin in the Church. (Hart and Bishop, "*Scivias,*" p. 172; italics in original)

Reflection

Hildegard named the virgin Mary mediatrix and salvatrix, a necessary instrument in the redemption of humankind. Although such a doctrine was often expressed in the twelfth century, Hildegard saw Mary's eminence reflect on all womanhood. God made a woman the mirror of God's beauty and the symbol of all creation.

Mary is also the new Eve. As a daughter of her time, Hildegard emphasized that woman caused humankind to fall, but she also declared that by woman, evil was overcome. Woman brought death through Eve, but death gave way because of Mary. According to Hildegard, Mary's simplicity does not separate her from the members of her sex, but bestows distinction upon them before the rest of creation. Mary is the *viriditas* and the flower hidden in every seed of being:

> . . . On the morn
>
> of the universe [God] saw you
> blossoming.
>
> You are the shining white lily
> on which God gazed
> before all creation.

(Newman, "*Symphonia,*" pp. 129, 123)

As the mother of God, Mary is the exemplar of a new creation. Through her maternity, Mary brings forth a new creation, which is like the first, only better. Through the Incarnation, she takes her place in the heart of God where all human beings belong. And so, Mary is the morning star who blazes the way for the dawning sun of justice.

✧ Ask yourself what your own devotion to Mary is like. What is special about her to you? Is she a real person, or have you "idealized" her out of your life? Do you pray to her regularly? Why or why not?

✧ Try to recall some traditional prayers to Mary that you learned as a child. You may wish to repeat some of them—for example, the Memorare, or Hail, Holy Queen, or the Angelus—as you ponder the imagery they contain. Do these images still console you? Challenge you? Invite you?

✧ Do you think anything about your own imagery of Mary should be changed? If so, you may wish to return to "Hildegard's Words" to see if any of Hildegard's images can help you.

✧ One of Hildegard's favorite symbols for Mary was the rising sun. Close your eyes and imagine a sunrise. Sit silently for a while wondering at this sunrise. Then ask yourself: What does this image bring to mind for me?

✧ Slowly read and pray the following verse from one of Hildegard's songs, and ponder the many images it contains:

Pierced by the light of God,
Mary Virgin,
drenched in the speech of God,
your body bloomed,
swelling with the breath of God.

(Newman, "*Symphonia*," p. 137)

After you have prayed and meditated on these verses, go back to the third line and substitute the phrase "speech of God" with the phrase "Word of God." Does a change of meaning happen? Which image pleases you more? Then, challenge yourself with this question: What would I be like if I were "drenched in the Word of God"? You may find writing your reflections helpful.

✧ In Eastern Christianity, Mary is honored with the title *theotokos,* which means "God bearer." As you prepare to reflect on the reading in "God's Word" given below, ponder for a few moments what it means for you to be a God bearer. How are you or can you be a God bearer where you work, in your relationships, with your family, or in your church?

God's Word

In the sixth month the angel Gabriel was sent by God to a town in Galilee called Nazareth, to a virgin betrothed to a man named Joseph, of the House of David; and the virgin's name was Mary. He went in and said to her, "Rejoice, you who enjoy God's favour! The Lord is with you." She was deeply disturbed by these words and asked herself what this greeting could mean, but the angel said to her, "Mary, do not be afraid; you have won God's favour. Look! You are to conceive in your womb and bear a son, and you must name him Jesus. He will be great and will be called Son of the Most High. . . . God will give him the throne of his ancestor David; he will rule over the House of Jacob for ever and his reign will have no end." Mary said to the angel, "But how can this come about, since I have no knowledge of man?" The angel answered, "The Holy Spirit will come upon you, and the power of the Most High will cover you with its shadow. And so the child will be holy and will be called Son of God. And I tell you this too: your cousin Elizabeth also, in her old age, has conceived a son, and she whom people called barren is now in her sixth month, for nothing is impossible to God." Mary said, "You see before you [God's] servant, let it happen to me as you have said." And the angel left her. (Luke 1:26–38)

Closing prayer: Hail, Mary, full of grace, God is with you. Blessed are you among women, and blessed is the fruit of your womb, Jesus. Holy Mary, mother of God, pray for us sinners, now and at the hour of our death. Amen.

✧ Meditation 14 ✧

Living with Conflict

Theme: Whenever Hildegard experienced the insight that comes from discerning God's will, she was filled with energy and refreshed in her zeal, even in difficult situations.

Opening prayer: "God, you are my shelter. I know that you will protect me from trouble and surround me with songs of liberation" (adapted from Psalm 32:7).

About Hildegard

Hildegard had her share of conflicts. As a gifted and active woman living in the Middle Ages, she had to struggle with the prevailing views of the time, which tended to keep women in their place. She had to wrestle with her feelings about recording her visions in writing. She needed to hear words of affirmation from Bernard of Clairvaux and church leaders. These were largely battles with herself. But Hildegard also struggled with others. One significant conflict she had influenced the course of her own life and of her nuns' life.

Along with Hildegard's growing fame came a steady stream of pilgrims to Saint Disibod. These visitors sought her counsel and also helped to increase the revenues of the women's and men's monasteries. Likewise, they brought many more new members to her community. Soon Hildegard felt that she and the nuns had outgrown their accommodations as well as their dependence on the monks. Thus, she decided to begin an independent foundation at Rupertsberg near Bingen. This decision prompted strong opposition from Abbot Kuno, who disliked the idea of losing not only the monastery's latest source of distinction but also the nuns' rich endowments. In protest, Abbot Kuno prohibited the monk Volmar, Hildegard's secretary, from moving to the new foundation with her. Also, some of the nuns were reluctant to leave their comfortable quarters for the insecurity of starting a new monastery. The local townspeople thought Hildegard was foolish for even thinking about a move.

Stressful as the situation was, Hildegard did not give up her plan. She enlisted the support of the archbishop of Mainz and, with the help of a rich countess, secured permission for the move and negotiated the acquisition of the land. Construction of the new monastery began swiftly, and in a short time, the nuns moved to the new quarters.

Despite this initial success, difficult days remained for Hildegard. Some dissatisfied nuns refused to enter the new monastery. Her closest friend, Richardis, left to become abbess of another monastery, and Hildegard's memoirs indicate that she felt abandoned and deeply betrayed, like Moses left wandering in the desert. Nevertheless, throughout the years at Rupertsberg, Hildegard continued her extensive correspondence and turned her creative energies to two vastly different fields: music and natural science.

The decade that followed saw the Rupertsberg monastery stabilize and free itself from the control of the monks, while Hildegard secured for the nuns a voice in the selection of a prioress. All during this time, she continued in almost boundless energy to produce creative works in prose and music.

Pause: Ponder this question: Where do I find strength to cope with the conflicts in my life?

Hildegard's Words

Hildegard's courage took root in her faith in God:

> For just as the sun is fixed in the firmament of heaven and has power over the creatures of the Earth so that nothing can overcome them, so also believers who have their hearts and minds directed toward God cannot be forgotten by God. (Fox, *Book of Divine Works,* p. 65)

Hildegard's faith led her to the conviction that God acts in all events, even in our struggles. She sent this advice to Archbishop Eberhard of Salzburg, who found himself caught in the struggle between his king and the pope:

> On the one hand, your desires and feelings sigh for the narrow path that leads to God. But, on the other hand, you have a whole realm of worries about the people entrusted to you. The former is in light; the latter in shadow.
> . . . You don't allow yourself to see that they belong together and this is why you so frequently experience depression in your spirit. For you fail to see your striving for God and your concern for people as a unity. . . .
>
> My counsel, therefore, father, is that you let your toil be saturated at the fountain of wisdom, there where the two daughters clothed with royal robes draw their water. And the names of these two royal daughters are "Love" and "Obedience." . . .
>
> . . . [I] see how your will longs for the door to these godly powers. This door will be open to you so that with these powers you can bring to fulfillment the difficult work assigned to you by Love. God who is and who fathoms all will support you both in your body and in your soul. (Fox, *Book of Divine Works,* pp. 283–285)

Reflection

Courage implies the resolve to meet danger with strength, daring, and confidence. Hildegard's decision to move to Rupertsberg had its own dangers that she had to face. Hers was not a selfish prudence that would risk nothing.

Hildegard's courage came from the conviction that God would uphold her if she followed God's will. She learned God's will through prayer and discernment of what love required of her. In other words, the light of wisdom shone when love motivated her and when she followed the light of love obediently.

✧ Ponder the most trying inner conflict that plagues you right now. If it helps, write a description of the conflict. Include all the elements: your feelings, each side of the conflict, external issues, and the history of how you dealt with similar conflicts in the past. What is your heart telling you to do? What is your head telling you? Go to a wise friend who will listen to the story of your inner conflict; tell her or him the story, and ask for any insights she or he might have. Finally, offer the conflict to the Holy Spirit. Ask for light, courage, and the patience needed to live through the conflict. Keep your heart, mind, and will open for the light of the Holy Spirit.

✧ Make a list of all the times you have acted courageously. Include acts of courage both large and small. Talk to Jesus about these times of courage and about his role in giving you strength.

✧ New beginnings can be both refreshing and draining. Jot down some new beginnings you have had to make in your life, and consider what your attitude was toward each.

Now, list one or two new beginnings you would like to initiate—maybe a new relationship, maybe a new attempt at reconciliation with an alienated friend, maybe a new project. Next to each new beginning, describe any fears you might have and then ways of coping with your fears. Finally, write a prayer, asking the Holy Spirit to send you the fire of strength you will need to make these new beginnings.

✧ Are you in the midst of a painful conflict with another person? Reflect on the relationship that is, at the moment, most worrisome for you. Then, imagine that you, the other person, and Jesus are sitting down together to talk about the conflict. Imagine that you are speaking to the person with whom you are at odds. Tell her or him what is bothering you.

Use "I" language—that is, own your own feelings, be descriptive, and do not throw blame on the other person. Some examples of statements that use "I" language are "When you said that I didn't care about you, I felt . . ." and "I get very angry when you say . . ."

When you have given your side of the conflict, imagine that you are the other person. Speak his or her side of the conflict. Be sure to use "I" language.

Next, invite Jesus to give his advice about resolving the conflict. Knowing what you do about the Good News, imagine what he would tell you.

Finally, when the imaginary conversation is over, determine a course of action to reconcile yourself with the other person.

✧ Slowly reread the two extracts in "Hildegard's Words" two or three times so that you can recall them throughout the day and be encouraged by what they say.

God's Word

In the world you will have hardship,
but be courageous:
I have conquered the world.

(John 16:33)

Closing prayer: God, I know that you are the God of all grace and that you have called me to eternal glory in Christ. Restore me, confirm me, strengthen and support me, and fill my heart with courage. Amen.

The Inner Glow of Peace

Theme: During her life, Hildegard knew the meaning of these words from Psalm 16, verse 11:

> You will show me the path that leads to life;
> your presence fills me with joy,
> and your help brings pleasure forever.

Opening prayer: God, I pray to know the peace that comes from trusting in you.

About Hildegard

Throughout her multifaceted life, Hildegard never ceased to be amazed at what God was working in her. As a wise woman of seventy-seven years, she expressed this wonder in a letter to Guibert of Gembloux. We are given a window into her soul as she reflected back on her life. She wrote:

> The words which I speak are not my own nor those of any human being, but what I say comes from the vision which I received from above. . . .
> From my childhood days, when my limbs, nerves, and veins were not yet strong, the gift of this vision brought joy to my soul; and this has remained true up to this very time when I am a woman of more than 70 years.

And as God wants, my soul climbs in this vision high above, even to the height of the firmament. But I do not see these things with my external eyes nor do I hear them with my external ears. I do not perceive them through the thoughts of my heart or through the mediation of my five senses. I see them much more in my soul alone, with my physical eyes open, in such a way that I never experience the unconsciousness of ecstasy, but I see all of this awake, whether by day or night.

The light which I see is not bound by space. It is much, much more light-filled than a cloud that carries the sun in itself. There is nothing in it to recognize of height, length, or breadth. It was described to me as the "shadow of the living light." And just as the sun, the moon, and the stars are reflected in water, so writings, talks, powers, and certain actions of people are illuminated for me in this light.

I was often severely hindered by sickness and involved with heavy sufferings that threatened to bring me to death's door. And yet God has always made me alive again, even to this day.

I keep for a long time in memory all the things I see and learn in the vision, because as soon as I see or hear it, it enters my memory. I simultaneously see, hear, and understand. In an instant I learn what I know through the vision. But whatever I do not see in the vision, I have no knowledge of, for I am without formal education and was only instructed to read simple letters. And I write what I see and hear in the vision and I don't add any other words. I communicate the plain Latin words just as I hear them in the vision. For I do not become educated in my vision so that I can write like the philosophers. The words in the vision do not sound like words from a human mouth, but they are like flaming lightning and like a cloud moving in the pure ether. I am not able to perceive the shape of this light, just as I cannot look with unprotected eyes at the disk of the sun.

It is in this light that I sometimes see, though not often, another light that I call "the living light." When and how I see this, I cannot say. But as long as I see this "living light" all sadness and anxiety are taken away from me. The result is that I feel like a simple young girl and not like an old lady. (Fox, *Book of Divine Works*, pp. 348–350)

Pause: Ask yourself: When have I experienced the inner glow of peace from being in harmony with God's wishes?

Hildegard's Words

In the youthful, ripening period of life, we come into complete flower. In old age, we are brought back to the period of fading, just as Earth in summer is adorned with flowers by its greening power and later transformed by the chill of winter's pallor.

When the soul overcomes the body in such a way that the body is in agreement with the soul in goodwill and simplicity of heart, and refreshed by good treatment as if by nourishing food, we cry out in our longing for heaven: "How sweet are the words of justice to my throat—even sweeter than honey to my mouth." And so we live in childish simplicity and a state of innocence without feeling the desires of the flesh. The soul floods us with its longing until, as we climb from virtue to virtue, we begin to feel a greening power. We start to bloom in the good works and examples left us by the Son of God. This is because we have not been stained by sin. And so we find joy and let ourselves be adorned. And just as the greening power and the flowering as well as the ripening of all fruits come to an end in winter, we also fade away at death along with all our good and evil works. Those of us, however, who have performed good works in our childhood, maturity, and old age will mount up with our soul to God, radiant in our good deeds and as if adorned with jewels. And the body by which the soul has done all these things will scarcely be able to wait until both body and soul are together again in the abode of joy. (Fox, *Book of Divine Works*, p. 113)

Reflection

Hildegard was energized by zeal right until the end of her days. Despite illness and the frailty of age, she continued to write and be busy at many projects. When she was seventy-nine, she wrote to Guibert: "There have been hindrances, for I am busy with some writing I have begun but have not yet finished. . . . Nevertheless, . . . I am happy to work further . . . as well as I can with God's help" (Fox, *Book of Divine Works*, p. 353). And she did.

The last two of Hildegard's letters to be preserved were written when she was in her eighty-first year. In them, we find her defending the burial of a young revolutionary in the cemetery at Rupertsberg and pleading for the lifting of the interdict that she and her sisters dutifully but painfully observed. This struggle between charism and structure was symbolic of her lifetime vocation as a prophetess. And in her steadfastness, we can understand why she was ultimately rewarded: she was empowered by the conviction that she was doing the work of God's justice. Shortly after she wrote these letters, the interdict was lifted, and Hildegard knew again, ever richer with the wisdom that comes with age, the inner glow of peace.

Despite all the struggles that crowd our life, God promises the inner glow of peace for us when we do the work of God's justice, hold steadfastly to God's word, and allow ourselves to be buoyed by God's love.

✧ Can any greater peace exist than to know one lives in the light and reflects back to others the brightness of God? From the life of Hildegard, we can learn that it is possible to know such peace. Can you think of any persons who have been such a "sage" to you? Are you especially fond of one in particular?

✧ Recall a few of the oldest people you know. Choose one or two and focus especially upon their face. If you have any photographs of them, you may wish to get those out so that you can intently gaze at them. What do the faces of these people tell you? How would you like to be known when you are their age? Are any of them now about Hildegard's age—that is, eighty-plus years? Perhaps resolve to speak with one of them in the immediate future. What might you hope to learn from her or him?

✦ Hildegard's words concerning aging tell us something about her. They reveal a woman who is obviously satisfied with her life. Even though we know she had to struggle with her own physical limitations and the restrictions placed on her as a woman by the structures of the time, we nonetheless are given the notion that Hildegard could look back at her life and name it good. She knew that her journey was worth the effort. Ponder your own life's journey. What can you learn about it from Hildegard?

✦ Hildegard marveled at God's constant love. Are you also amazed at what God has wrought in your life? Compose a list of some astonishing and marvelous events in your life. Ponder each event; savor it. Carry the memory of these graced times with you today and make of them a prayer of praise and thanksgiving.

God's Word

When my heart had been growing sour
and I was pained in my innermost parts,
I had been foolish and misunderstood;
. . . .
Nevertheless, I waited in your presence;
you grasped my right hand.
Now guide me with your counsel
and receive me into glory at last.

(Psalm 73:21–24)

Closing prayer: I pray now with Hildegard:

Holy Spirit, making life alive,
moving in all things, root of all created being,
. . . .
You are lustrous and praiseworthy life,
You waken and re-awaken everything that is.

(Fox, *Book of Divine Works*, p. 373)

May I never forget your sustaining presence no matter what I experience from the outside. Throughout all my days, may I know the inner glow of your abiding peace. Amen. Alleluia!

LIGHT

✧ For Further Reading ✧

Books

Fox, Matthew, ed. *Hildegard of Bingen's Book of Divine Works with Letters and Songs.* Santa Fe, NM: Bear and Company, 1987.

Hart, Mother Columba, and Jane Bishop, trans. *Hildegard of Bingen, "Scivias."* New York: Paulist Press, 1990.

Newman, Barbara. *Sister of Wisdom.* Berkeley: University of California Press, 1987.

Strehlow, Dr. Wighard, and Gottfried Hertzka. *Hildegard of Bingen's Medicine.* Santa Fe, NM: Bear and Company, 1990.

Recordings

A Feather on the Breath of God: Sequences and Hymns by Hildegard of Bingen. Gothic Voices, directed by Christopher Page. Hyperion A66039, recorded in London, 1982. Musical Heritage Society selection for 1984.

Gesange der hl. Hildegard von Bingen. Schola der Benediktinerinnenabtei Saint Hildegard, directed by M. I. Ritscher. Psallite 242/040 479 PET, recorded in West Germany, 1969. May be ordered directly from the Abbey of Saint Hildegard, 6220 Rudesheium-Eibingen/Rhein, Postfach 13 20, Germany.

Hildegard von Bingen: Symphoniae (Geistliche Gesange). Sequentia, directed by Barbara Thornton and Margriet Tindemans. Deutsche Harmonia Mundi 19 9976 1, recorded in Cologne, 1985.

Acknowledgments (*continued*)

The psalms quoted in this book are from *Psalms Anew: In Inclusive Language,* compiled by Nancy Schreck and Maureen Leach (Winona, MN: Saint Mary's Press, 1986). Copyright © 1986 by Saint Mary's Press. Used with permission. All rights reserved.

The scriptural material found on pages 35–36, 64, 80, and 99 is freely adapted to make it inclusive regarding gender. These adaptations are not to be understood or used as official translations of the Bible.

All other scriptural quotations used in this book are from the New Jerusalem Bible. Copyright © 1985 by Darton, Longman & Todd, Ltd.,London, and Doubleday, a division of Bantam, Doubleday, Dell Publishing Group, Inc., New York. Used with permission.

The excerpts on pages 15, 71–72, and 89 are from *Sister of Wisdom: St. Hildegard's Theology of the Feminine,* by Barbara Newman (Berkeley, CA: The University of California Press, 1987), pages 1–2, 69–70, and 180, respectively. Copyright © 1987 by the Regents of the University of California. Used with permission.

The excerpts on pages 18, 59–60, and 71 are from *"Saint Hildegard of Bingen,"* by Sister Anna Silvas, in *Tjurunga: An Australasian Benedictine Review* (Australia: The Benedictine Union of Australasia), volume 31, pages 37, 40, and 39, respectively. Used with permission.

The excerpts on pages 21, 28–29, 47–48, 54, 77, 78–79, 83, and 95 are from *Hildegard of Bingen: "Scivias,"* translated by Mother Columba Hart and Jane Bishop (New York: Paulist Press, 1990), pages 59, 59–60, 467, 405, 529, 442–443, 123, and 172, respectively. Copyright © 1990 by the Abbey of Regina Laudis: Benedictine Congregation Regina Laudis of the Strict Observance, Inc. Used by permission of Paulist Press.

The excerpts on pages 22, 25, 26, and 38 are from *"Translation: The Life of Saint Hildegard,"* by Sister Anna Silvas, in *Tjurunga: An Australasian Benedictine Review* (Australia: The Benedictine Union of Australasia), volume 29, pages 25, 12, 15, and 23, respectively. Used with permission.

Titles in the Companions for the Journey Series

Praying with Anthony of Padua
Praying with Benedict
Praying with Catherine McAuley
Praying with Catherine of Siena
Praying with Clare of Assisi
Praying with Dominic
Praying with Dorothy Day
Praying with Elizabeth Seton
Praying with Francis de Sales
Praying with Francis of Assisi
Praying with Frédéric Ozanam
Praying with Hildegard of Bingen
Praying with Ignatius of Loyola
Praying with John Baptist de La Salle
Praying with John Cardinal Newman
Praying with John of the Cross
Praying with Julian of Norwich
Praying with Louise de Marillac
Praying with Teresa of Ávila
Praying with Thérèse of Lisieux
Praying with Thomas Merton
Praying with Vincent de Paul

Order from your local religious bookstore or from

Saint Mary's Press
702 TERRACE HEIGHTS
WINONA MN 55987-1320
USA
1-800-533-8095